ROD STEWART
GUITAR ANTHOLOGY

RECORDED VERSIONS GUITAR
AUTHENTIC TRANSCRIPTIONS WITH NOTES AND TABLATURE

Cover photo by Robert Knight

Music transcriptions by Ron Piccione

ISBN 978-1-4234-3989-9

HAL•LEONARD® CORPORATION

7777 W. BLUEMOUND RD. P.O. BOX 13819 MILWAUKEE, WI 53213

Visit Hal Leonard Online at
www.halleonard.com

from *Blondes Have More Fun*

Da Ya Think I'm Sexy

Words and Music by Rod Stewart and Carmine Appice

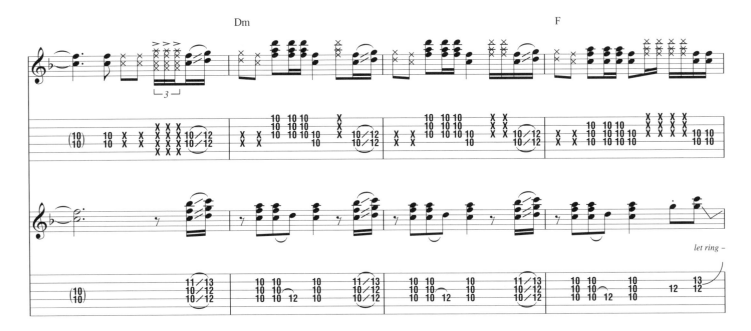

*Chord symbols reflect overall harmony.

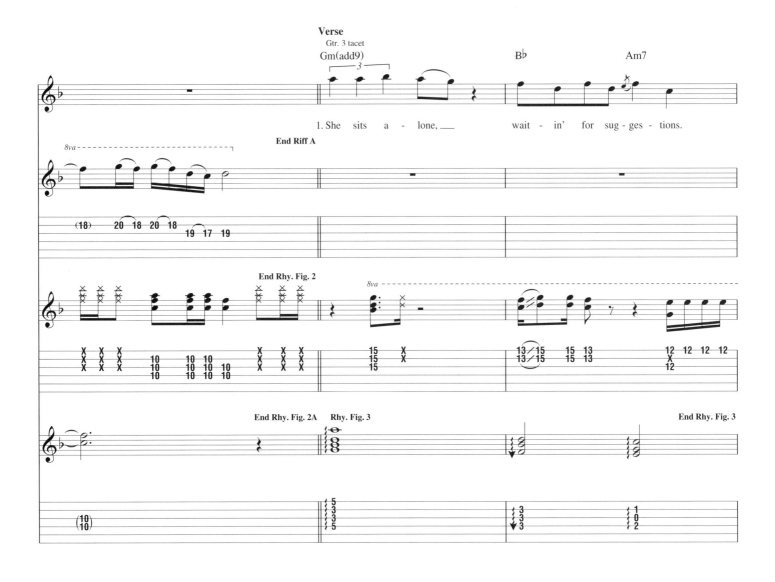

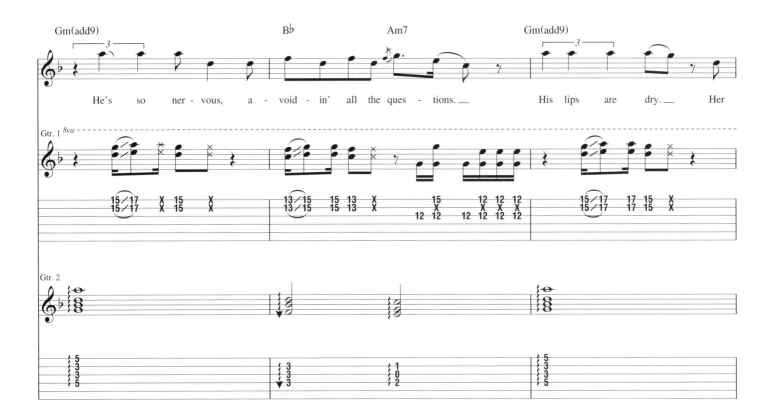

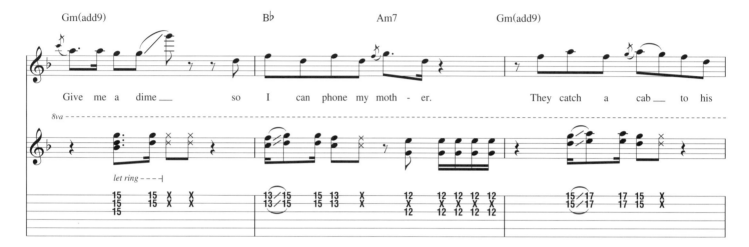

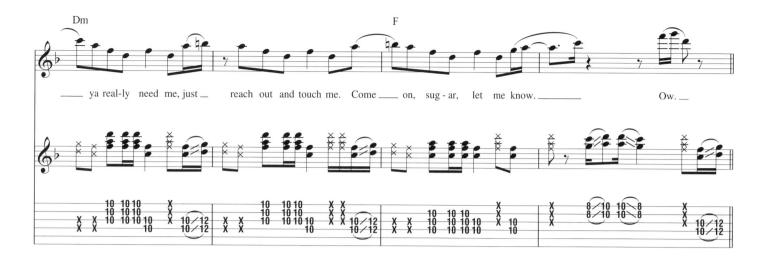

_ya real-ly need me, just _ reach out and touch me. Come _ on, sug - ar, let me know. _ Ow. _

Interlude

Gtr. 2: w/ Rhy. Fig. 2A
Gtr. 3: w/ Riff A

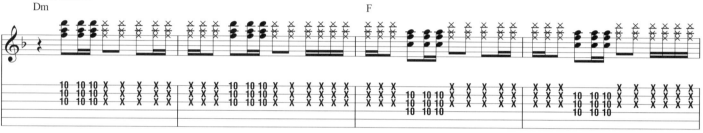

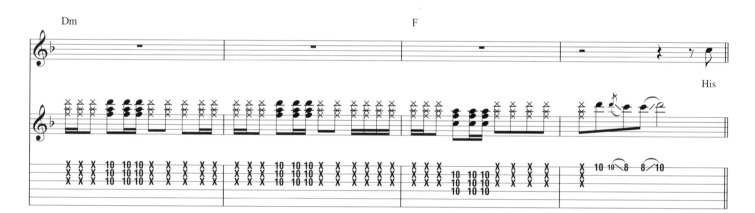

His

Bridge

heart's _ beat - in' like a drum _ 'cause at last he's got this girl _ home. _

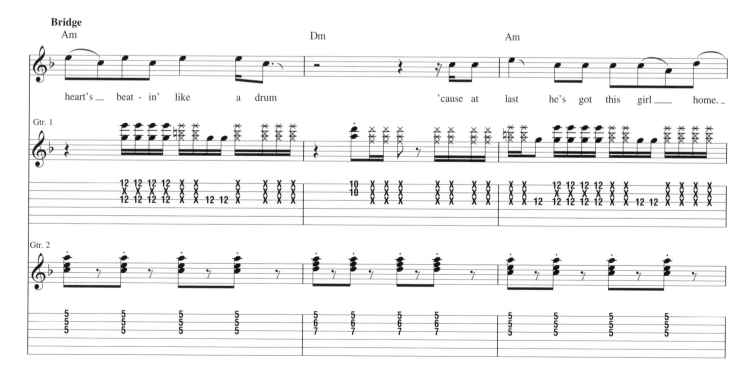

9

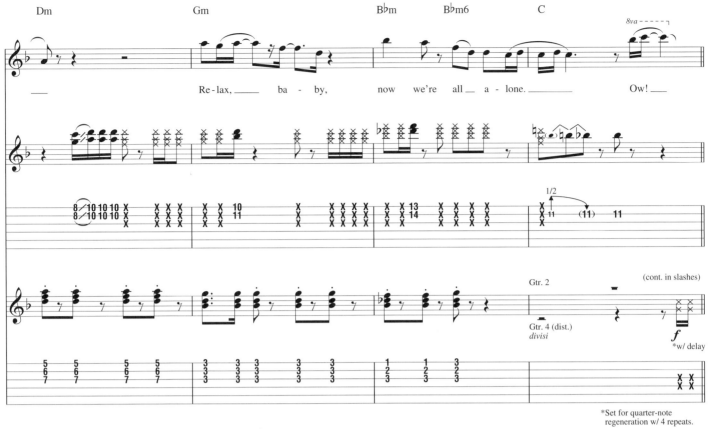

Re-lax, _____ ba - by, now we're all _____ a - lone. _____ Ow! _____

*Set for quarter-note
regeneration w/ 4 repeats.

Saxophone Solo

**Saxophone arr. for gtr.

*See top of first page of song for chord diagrams pertaining to rhythm slashes.

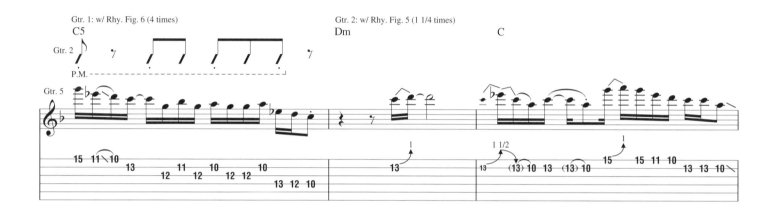

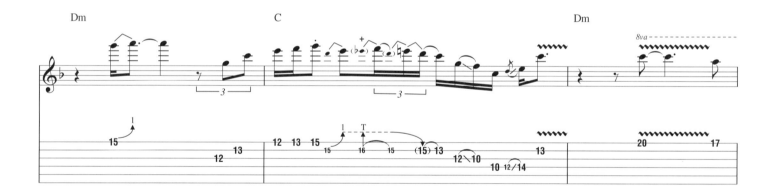

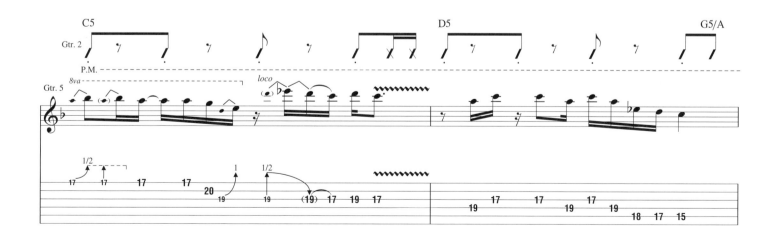

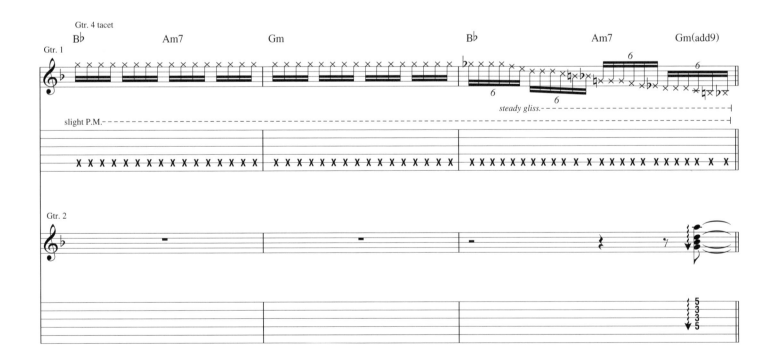

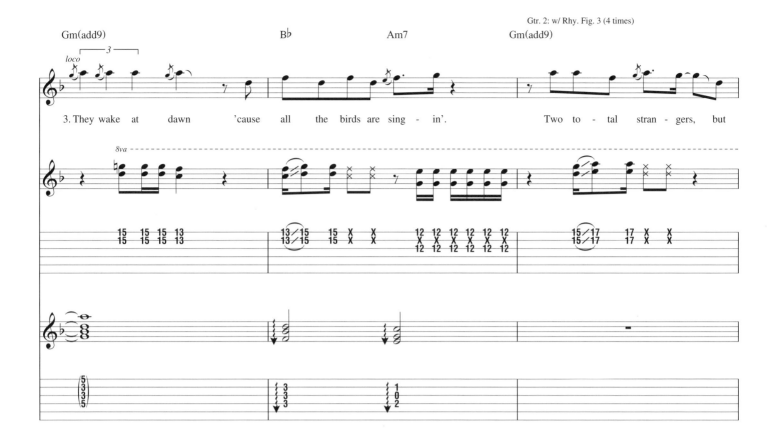

3. They wake at dawn 'cause all the birds are sing - in'. Two to - tal stran - gers, but

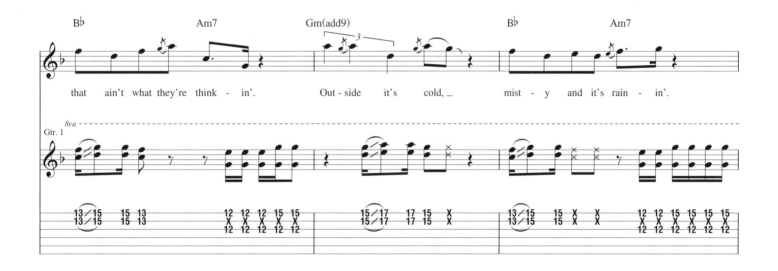

that ain't what they're think - in'. Out - side it's cold, __ mist - y and it's rain - in'.

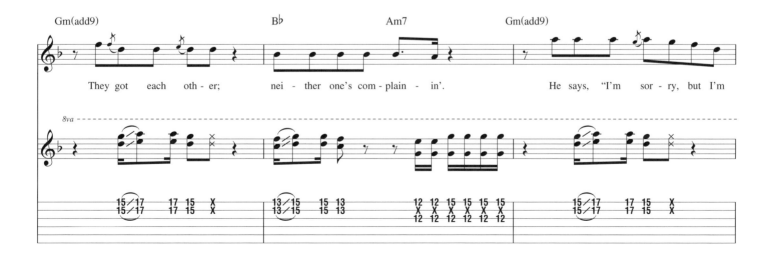

They got each oth - er; nei - ther one's com - plain - in'. He says, "I'm sor - ry, but I'm

out of milk and cof - fee." Nev - er mind, sug - ar, we can watch the ear - ly mov - ie. If

Outro-Chorus

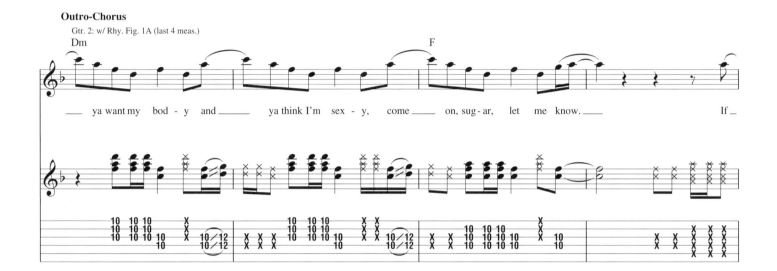

Gtr. 2: w/ Rhy. Fig. 1A (last 4 meas.)

___ ya want my bod - y and ___ ya think I'm sex - y, come ___ on, sug - ar, let me know. ___ If ___

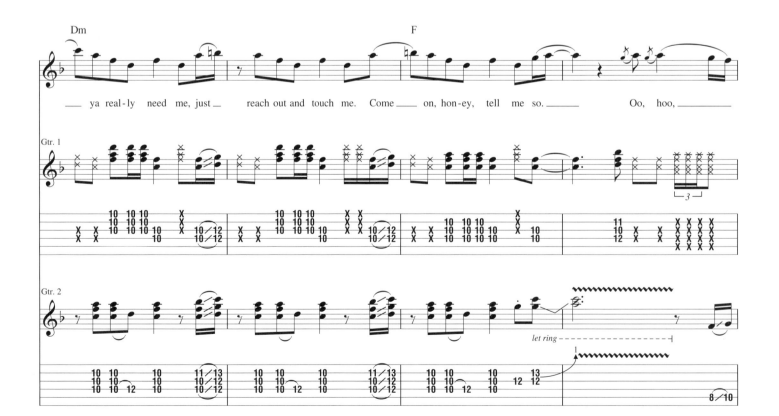

___ ya real - ly need me, just ___ reach out and touch me. Come ___ on, hon - ey, tell me so. ___ Oo, hoo, ___

Outro

Gtr. 3: w/ Riff A (till fade)

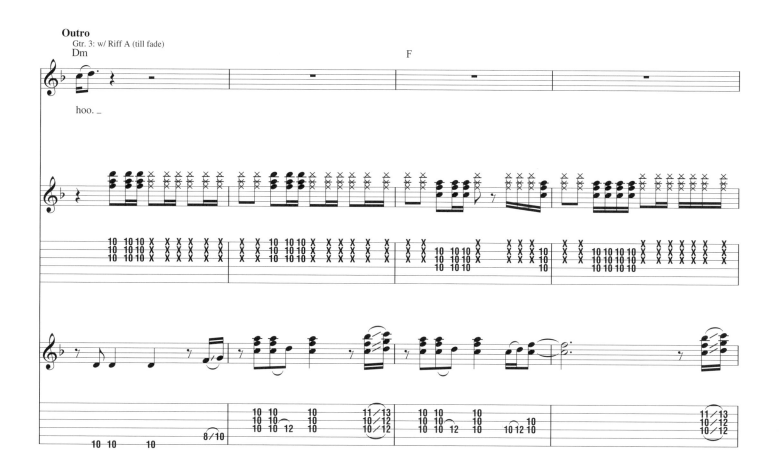

hoo.

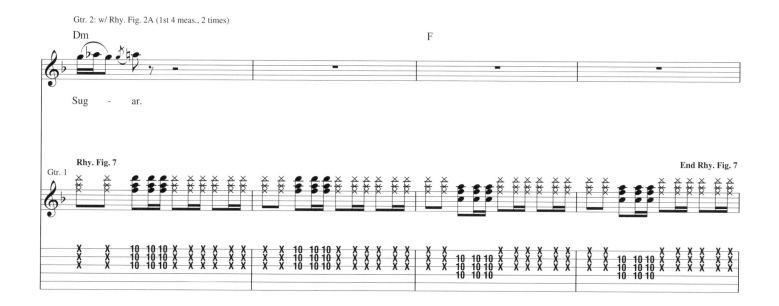

Gtr. 2: w/ Rhy. Fig. 2A (1st 4 meas., 2 times)

Sug - ar.

Rhy. Fig. 7

Gtr. 1

End Rhy. Fig. 7

Gtr. 1: w/ Rhy. Fig. 7 (till fade)

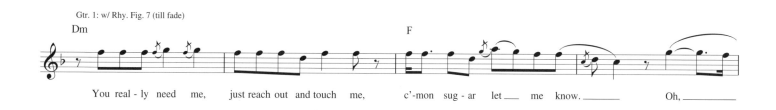

You real - ly need me, just reach out and touch me, c'-mon sug - ar let __ me know. _____ Oh, _____

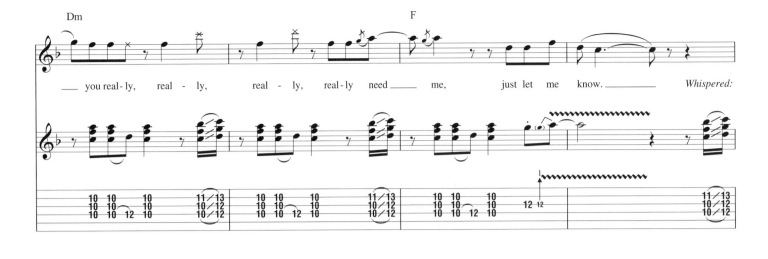

_you real-ly, real - ly, real - ly, real - ly need ____ me, just let me know. ____ *Whispered:*

Gtr. 2: w/ Rhy. Fig 2A (1st 4 meas., 3 times)

Just reach out and touch me.   Mm. ____   *Whispered:* If ____

____ you real - ly want me,   just reach out and touch me,   c'-mon, sug - ar let me know. ____

If you real - ly need ___ me, ja, just reach out and touch me,   c'- mon sug - ar, let ____ me know.   If ____

Begin fade

____ you, if ____ you, if ____ you real-ly need me, just ____ come on and tell ____ me so. ____   Mm,   mm. ____

Fade out

Gtr. 2: w/ Rhy. Fig. 2A (1st 4 meas.)

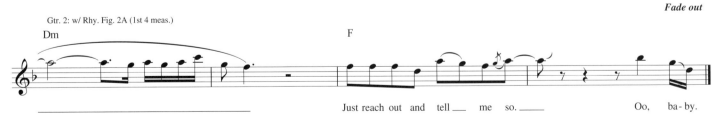

Just reach out and tell ____ me so. ____   Oo,   ba - by.

Every Picture Tells a Story

Words and Music by Rod Stewart and Ron Wood

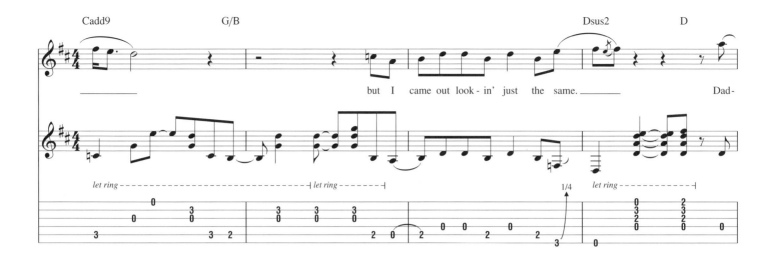

but I came out look-in' just the same. _____ Dad-

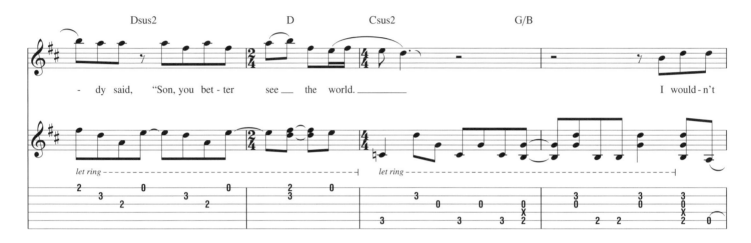

- dy said, "Son, you bet-ter see ___ the world. _____ I would-n't

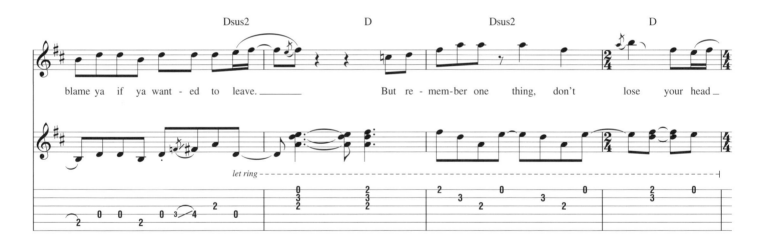

blame ya if ya want-ed to leave. _____ But re-mem-ber one thing, don't lose your head ___

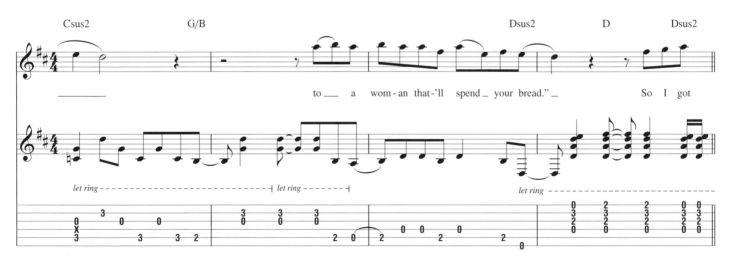

to ___ a wom-an that-'ll spend ___ your bread." ___ So I got

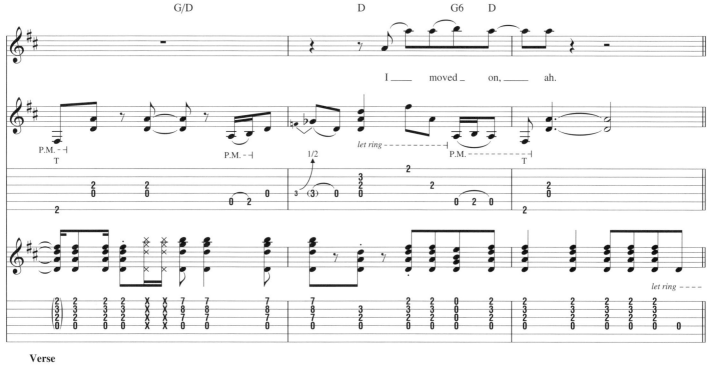

I ____ moved ____ on, ____ ah.

Verse

Gtr. 2 tacet

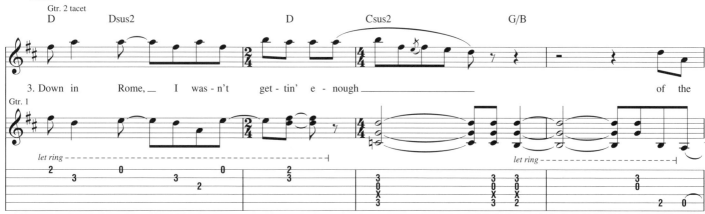

3. Down in Rome, ___ I was-n't get-tin' e - nough _____ of the

Gtr. 1

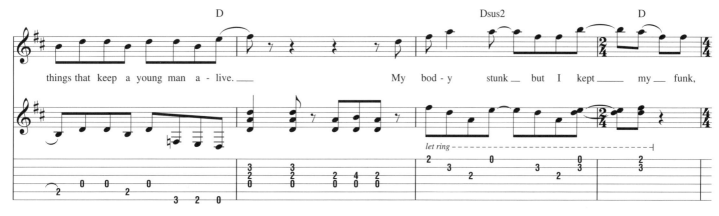

things that keep a young man a - live. ____ My bod-y stunk ___ but I kept ___ my ___ funk,

woo, ____ at ___ a time when I was right out-ta luck.

Get-tin' des-p'rate, in-deed I ___ was, ___ yeah, you're
look-in' like a tour-ist at-trac - tion. Oh, my dear, _ I bet-ter get out-ta here, _
for _ the Vat-i-can don't give no _ sanc - tion. I was-n't
read-y for that, no, no.

Interlude

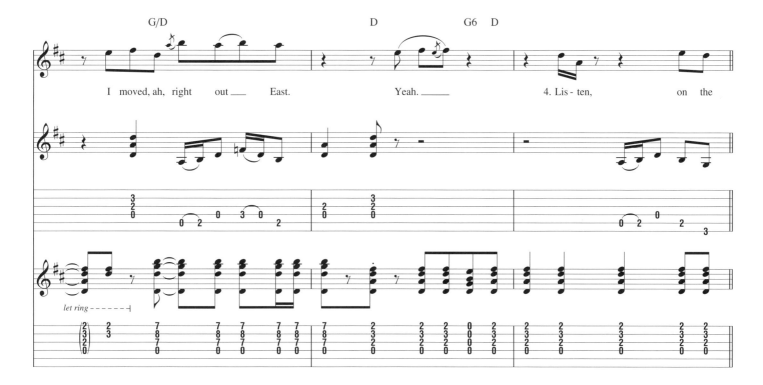

I moved, ah, right out ___ East. Yeah. ___ 4. Lis - ten, on the

Verse

Pe - king fer - ry, I was feel - ing ___ mer - ry,

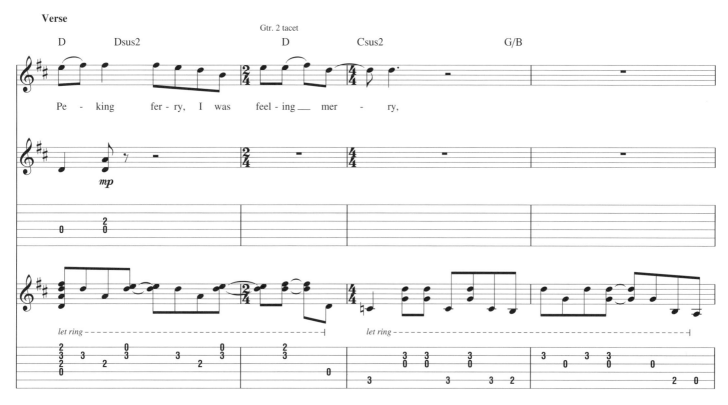

sail - ing on my way back here. ___ I feel in love ___ with a slit - eyed ___ la -

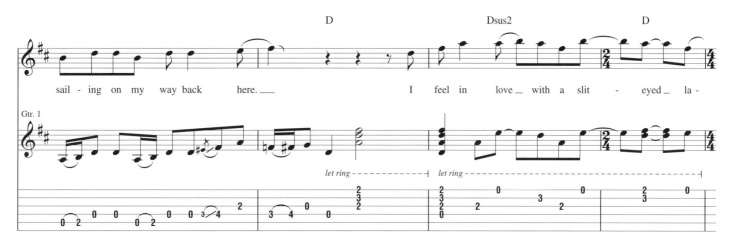

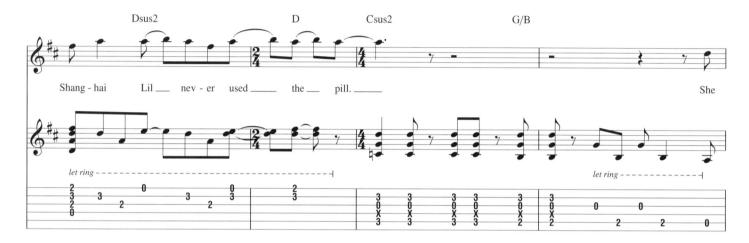

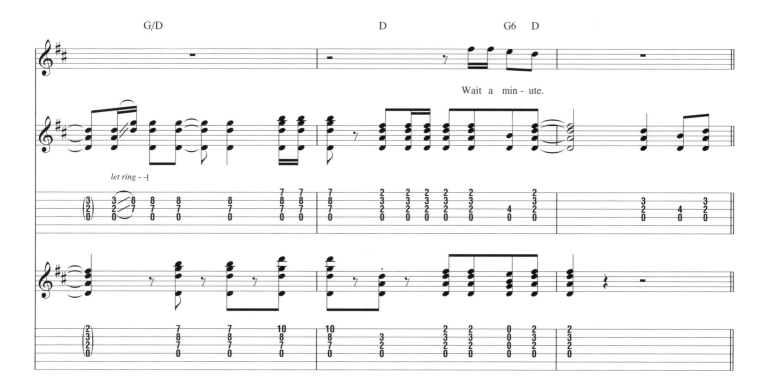

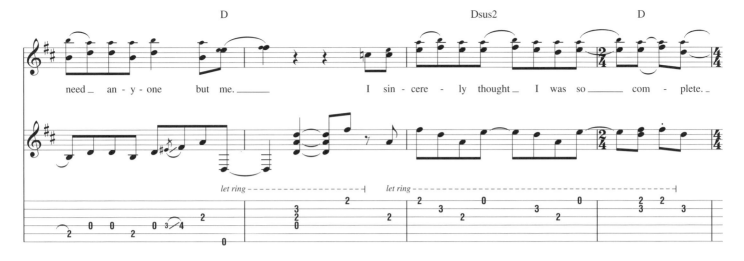

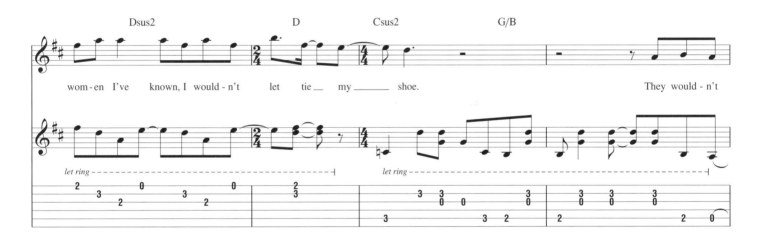

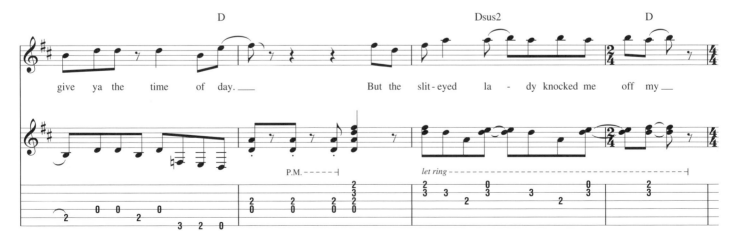

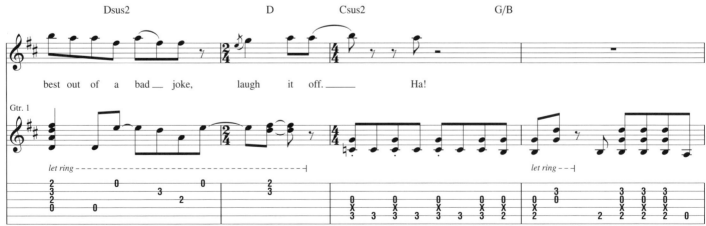

*See top of first page of song for chord
diagram pertaining to rhythm slash.

Outro-Chorus

Gtr. 2

Gtr. 1

**Chord symbol reflects basic harmony.

pic - ture tells a sto - ry, don't ___ it? Woo!_ Ev - 'ry pic - ture tells a sto - ry, don't ___ it? Ev - 'ry

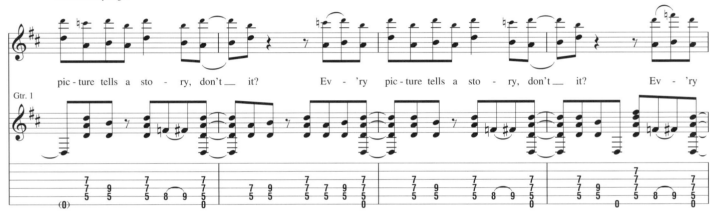

Gtr. 2: w/ Rhy. Fig. 1

pic - ture tells a sto - ry, don't ___ it? Ev - 'ry pic - ture tells a sto - ry, don't ___ it? Ev - 'ry

pic - ture tells a sto - ry, don't ___ it? Ev - 'ry pic - ture tells a sto - ry. Woo, _____ hoo.
(Ev - 'ry pic - ture tells a sto - ry, don't ___ it? Ev - 'ry)

(Ev - 'ry pic - ture tells a sto - ry, don't _____ it? Ev - 'ry)

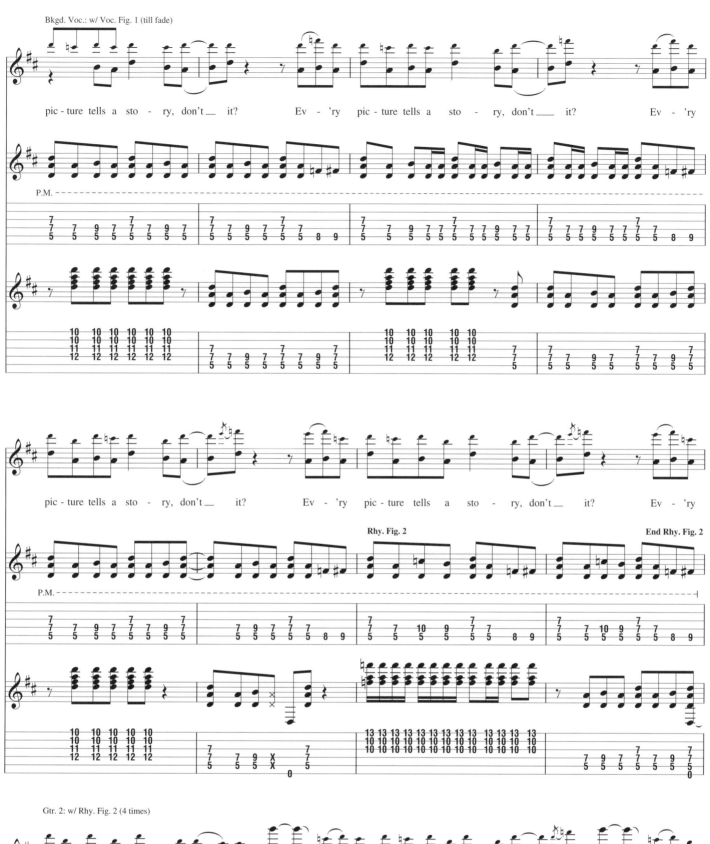

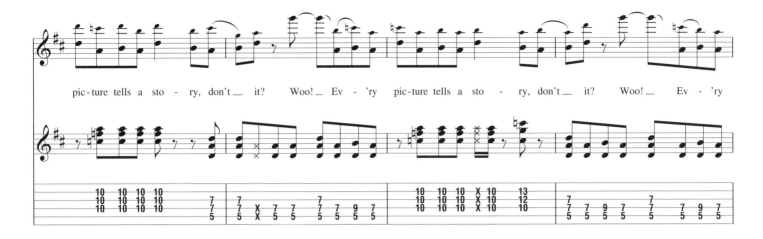

pic - ture tells a sto - ry, don't __ it? Woo! __ Ev - 'ry pic - ture tells a sto - ry, don't __ it? Woo! __ Ev - 'ry

Begin fade

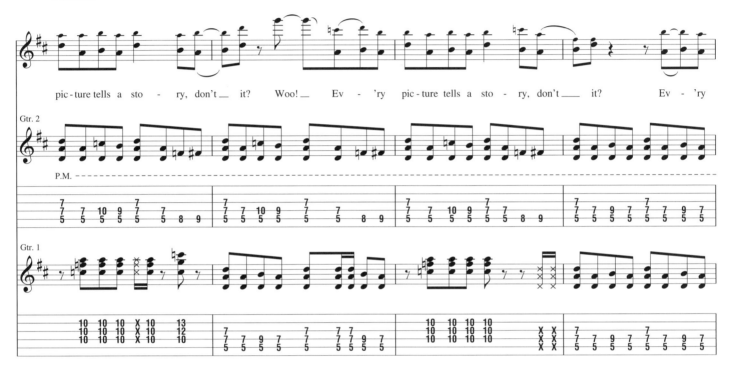

pic - ture tells a sto - ry, don't __ it? Woo! __ Ev - 'ry pic - ture tells a sto - ry, don't ___ it? Ev - 'ry

Gtr. 2

Gtr. 1

Fade out

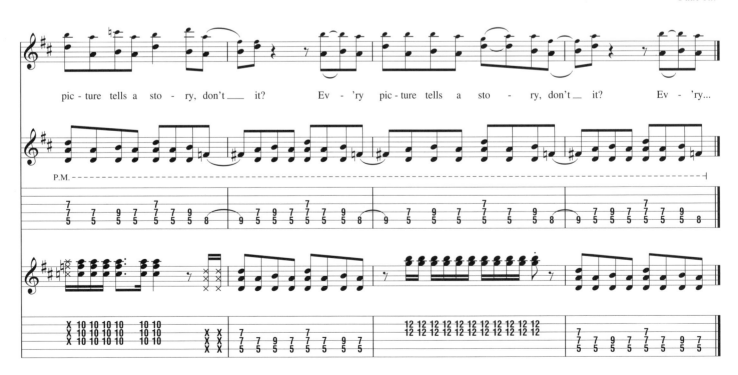

pic - ture tells a sto - ry, don't ___ it? Ev - 'ry pic - ture tells a sto - ry, don't __ it? Ev - 'ry...

from *A Night on the Town*

The First Cut Is the Deepest

Words and Music by Cat Stevens

1. I would have

Verse

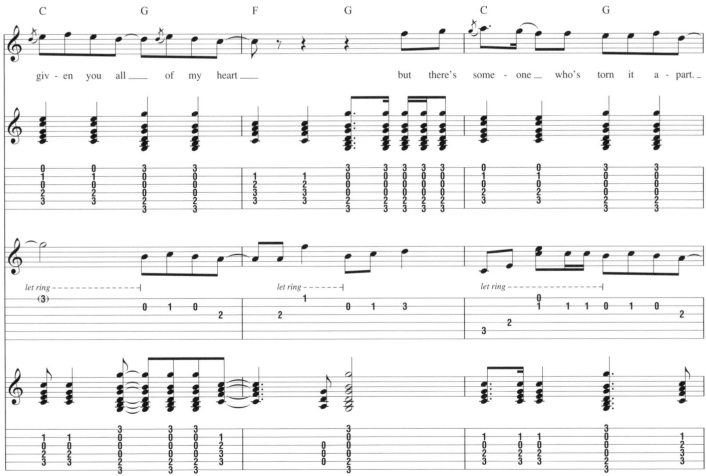

giv - en you all ___ of my heart ___ but there's some - one ___ who's torn it a - part. ___

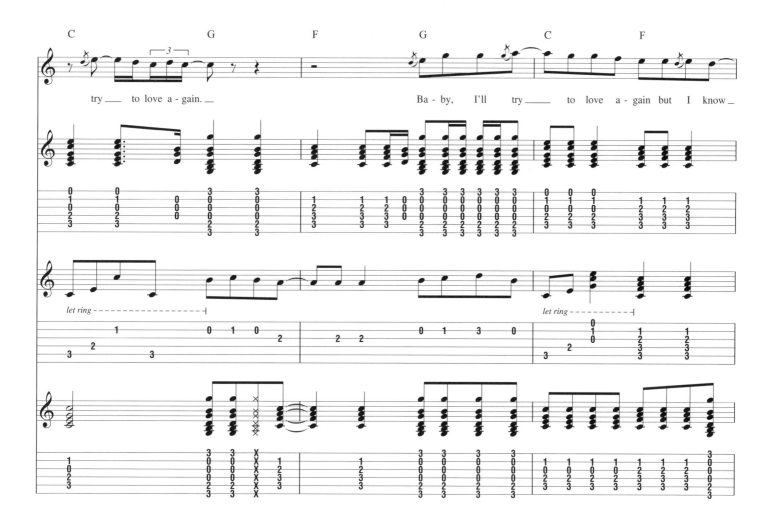

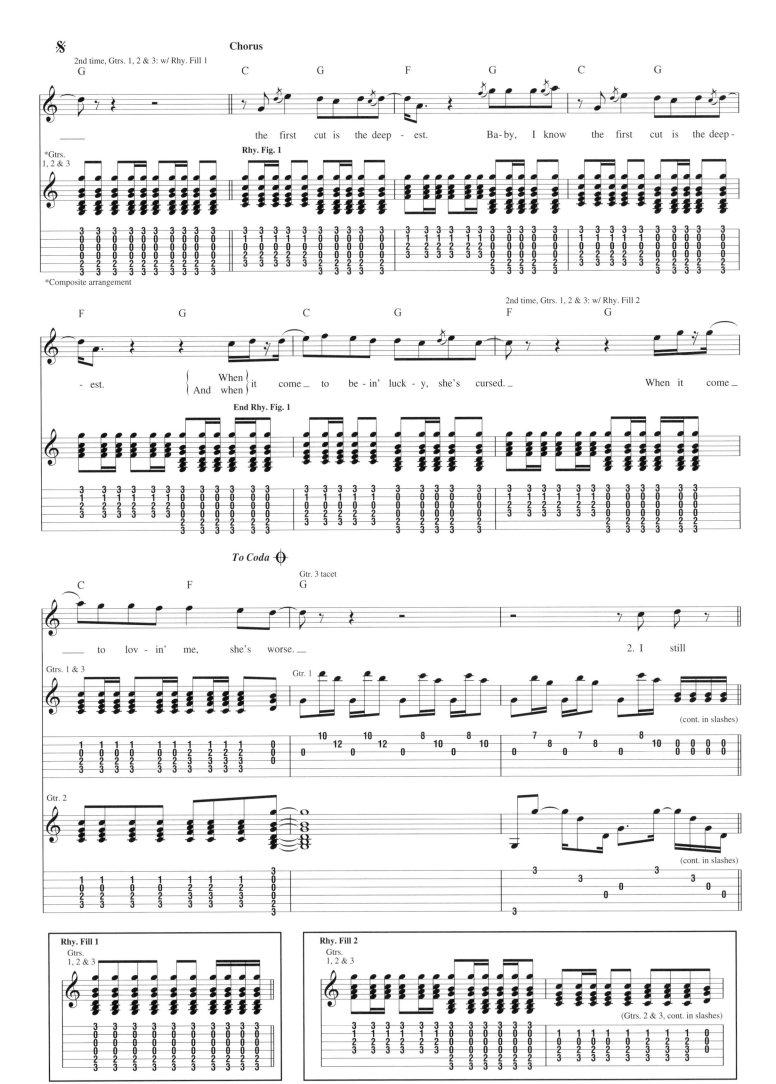

Verse

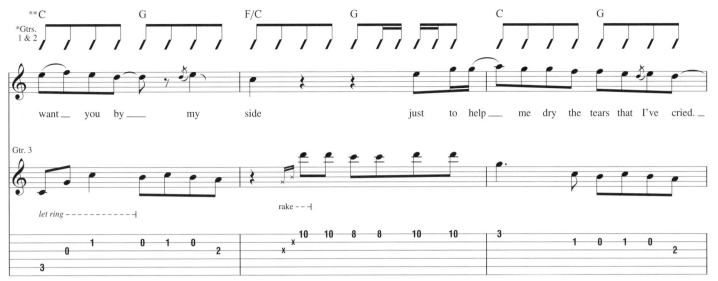

want __ you by __ my side just to help __ me dry the tears that I've cried. __

*Composite arrangement

**See top of first page of song for chord diagrams pertaining to rhythm slashes.

__ And I'm sure gon-na give you a try. __ And, if __ you want, I'll

D.S. al Coda

try to love a-gain. __ Ba - by, I'll try __ to love a-gain but I know __

from *Out of Order*

Forever Young

Words and Music by Rod Stewart, Kevin Savigar, Jim Cregan and Bob Dylan

†w/ echo set for quarter-note regeneration w/ 3 repeats.

sun-shine and hap-pi-ness __ sur-round you when you're far __ from home. __

And may you

*As before

grow __ to be proud, __ dig-ni-fied, __ and true. __

And

**As before

do un-to oth-ers as you would have done __ to you. __

Be cou-

***As before

Pre-Chorus

Gtr. 1 tacet

F#m

A

C#m

A

ra - geous and __ be brave, __ and in __ my heart __ you'll al - ways __ stay __ for - ev - er

Chorus

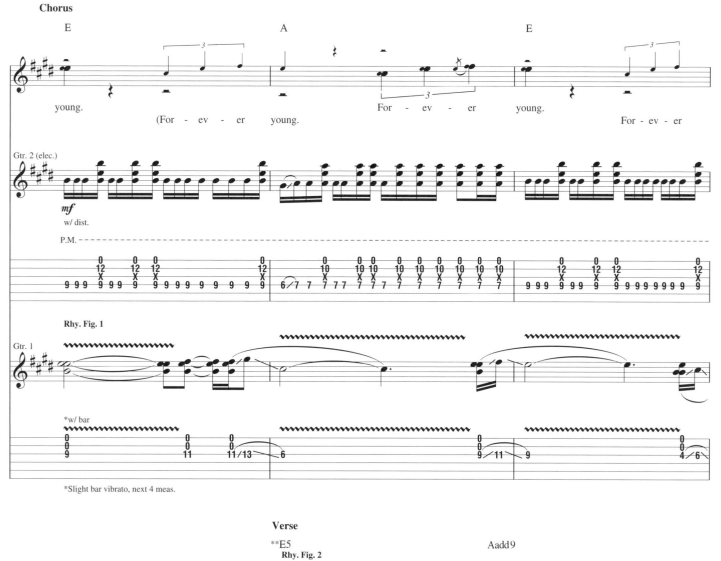

*Slight bar vibrato, next 4 meas.

Verse

**See top of first page of song for chord diagrams pertaining to rhythm slashes.

***As before

Build a stair - way_ to heav - en with a

prince or a vag - a - bond. ____ And may you

Pre-Chorus

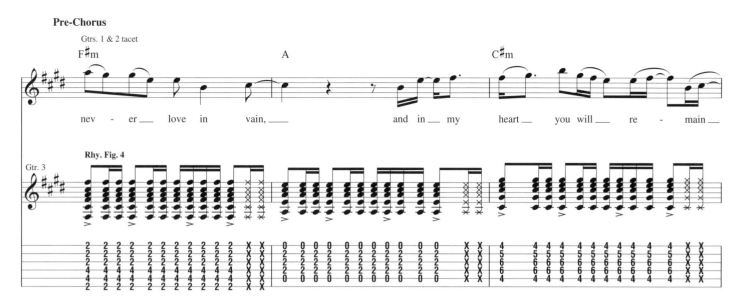

never love in vain, and in my heart you will re-main

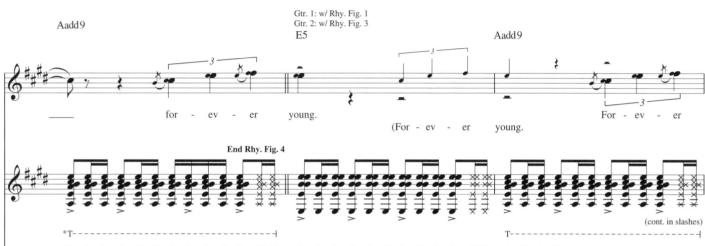

Chorus

Gtr. 1: w/ Rhy. Fig. 1
Gtr. 2: w/ Rhy. Fig. 3

for - ev - er young.

(For - ev - er young. For - ev - er

young. For - ev - er young.) For - ev - er

(For - ev - er

Verse

Gtr. 2: w/ Rhy. Fig. 3 (2 times)
Gtr. 3: w/ Rhy. Fig. 2
Gtr. 4 tacet

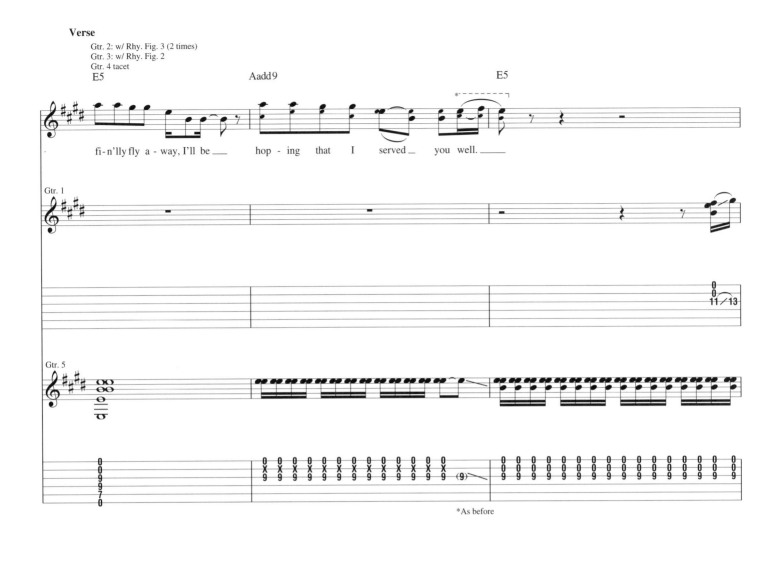

fi-n'lly fly a - way, I'll be ___ hop - ing that I served ___ you well. ___

*As before

For all ___ the wis-dom of ___ a life - time, no one can ev - er tell. ___

**As before

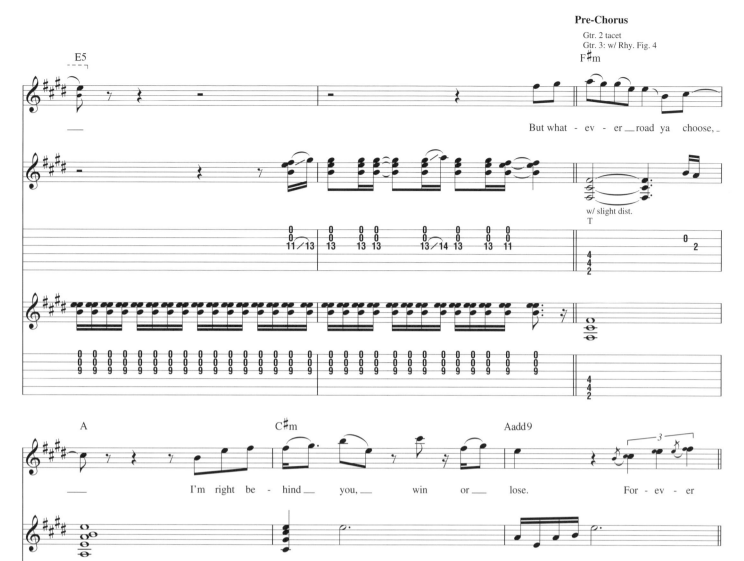

But what - ev - er ___ road ya choose, ___

w/ slight dist.

I'm right be - hind ___ you, ___ win or ___ lose.

For - ev - er

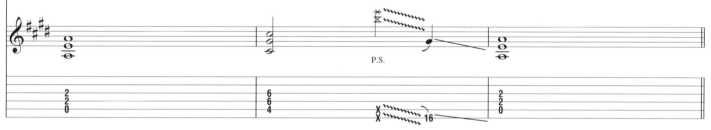

Outro-Chorus
Gtr. 1: w/ Rhy. Fig. 1
Gtr. 2: w/ Rhy. Fig. 3
Gtr. 3: w/ Rhy. Fig. 2 (last 4 meas.)

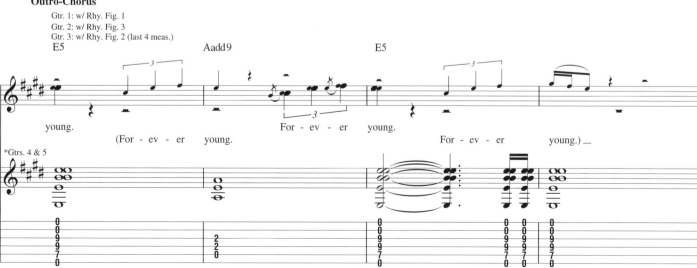

young.

(For - ev - er young.)

For - ev - er young.

For - ev - er young.) ___

*Gtrs. 4 & 5

*Composite arrangement

Gasoline Alley

Words and Music by Rod Stewart and Ron Wood

Chorus

Verse

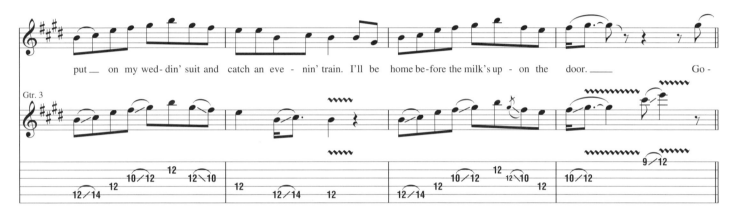

Chorus

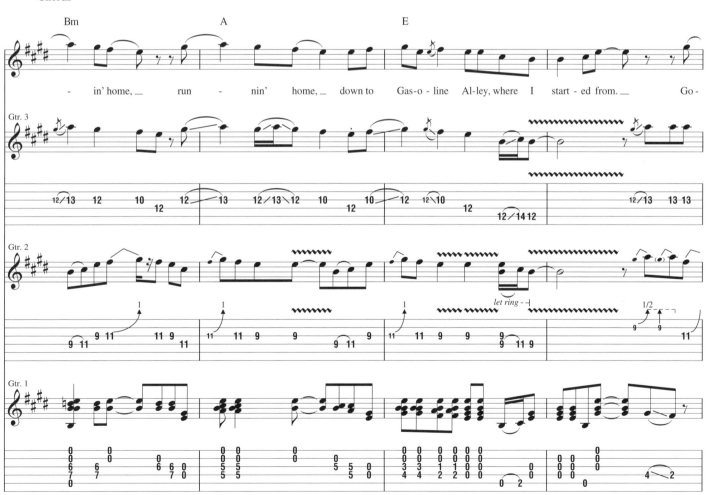

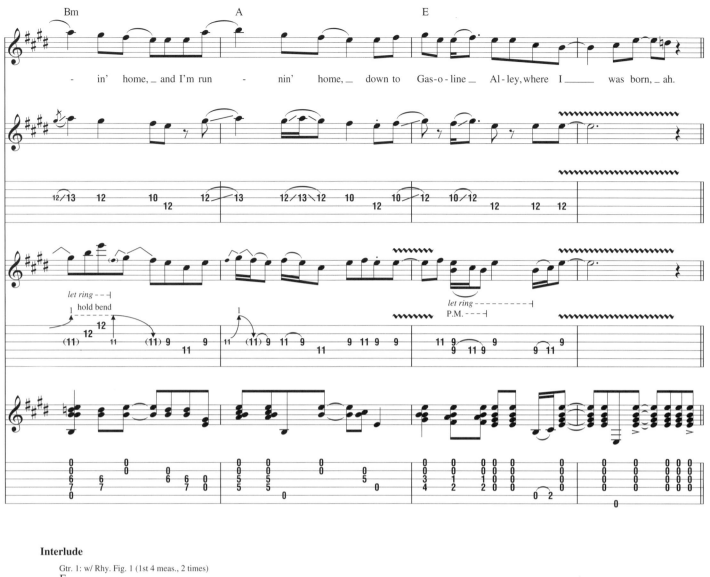

Interlude

Gtr. 1: w/ Rhy. Fig. 1 (1st 4 meas., 2 times)

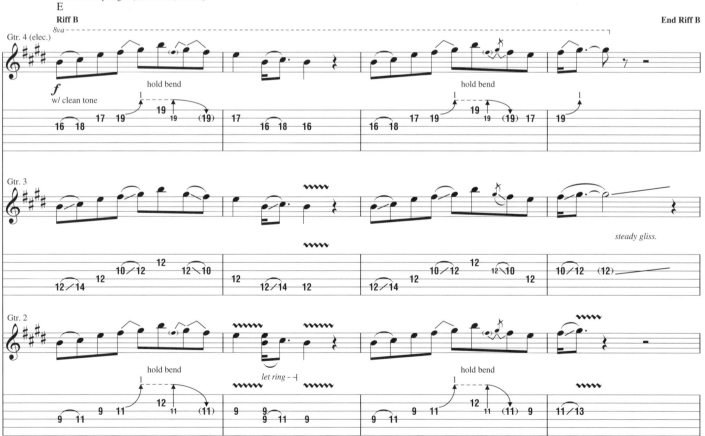

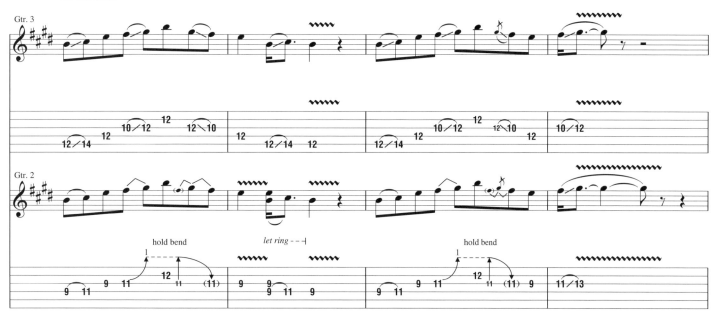

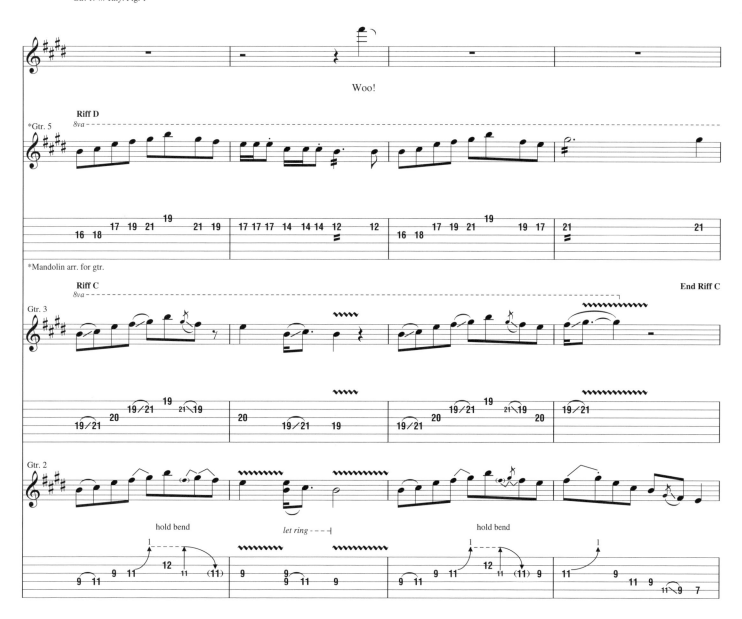

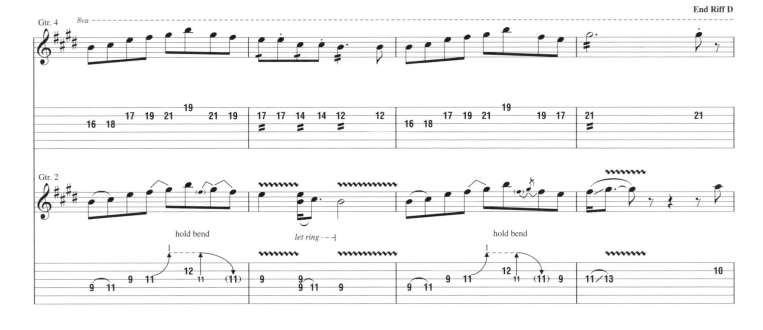

Verse

Gtr. 1: w/ Rhy. Fig. 1 (1st 4 meas., 3 times)
Gtr. 5: w/ Riff D (1 1/2 times)

an - y-thing should hap-pen and my plans go __ wrong, should I stray __ to the house __ on the hill? _____

_____ me back, _ car - ry me back _ down to Gas-o-line _ Al-ley, where I start-ed from. _ Take _

64

me back, ___ car - ry me back _ down to Gas-o-line _ Al - ley, where I start - ed from. _ Take _

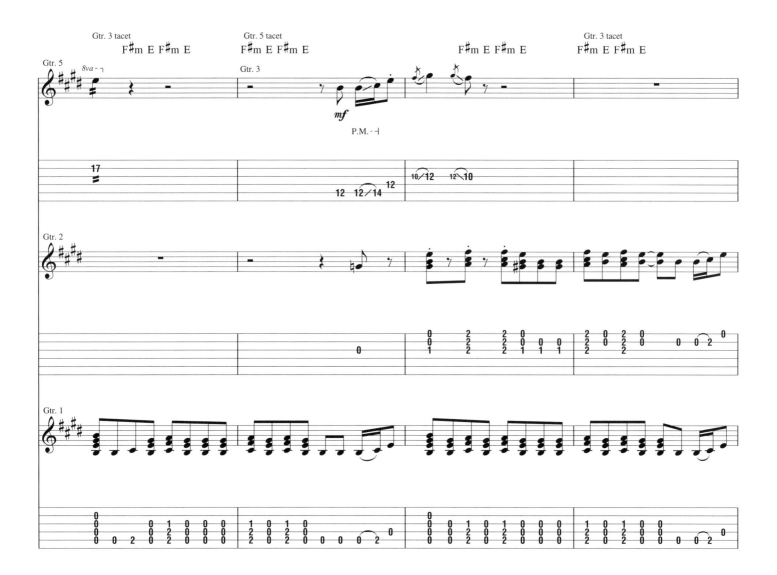

Free Time

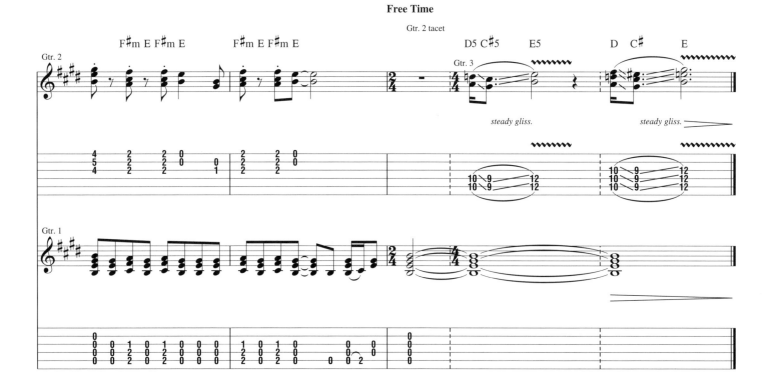

Hot Legs

Words and Music by Rod Stewart

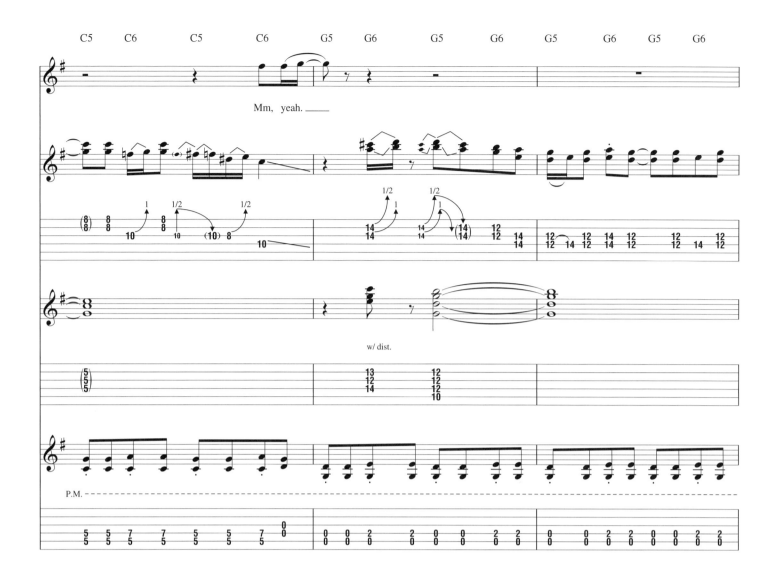

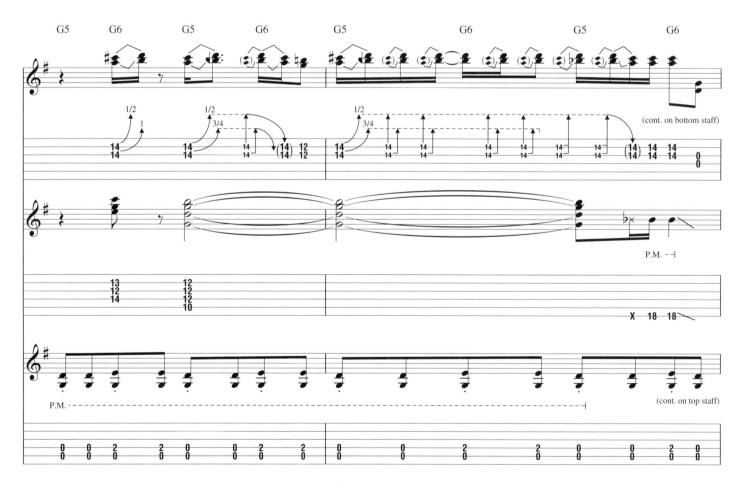

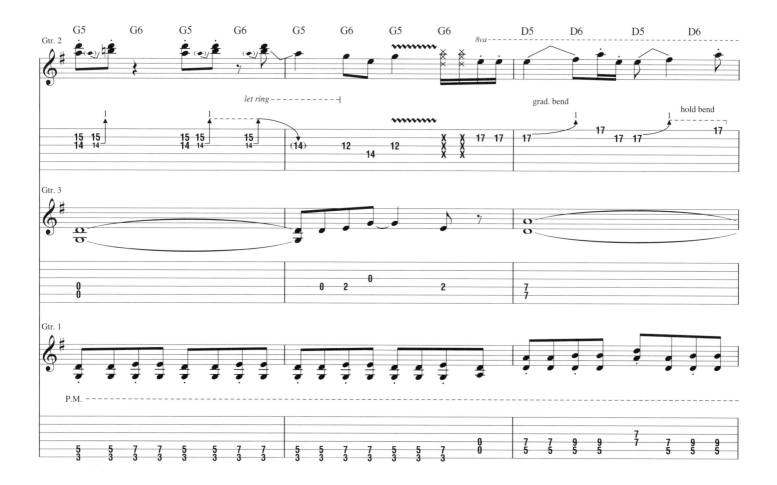

§ **Verse**

1. Who's __ that __ knock-in' on the door? __ It's got-ta be a quart-er to four. __
3. 'Mag-ine how my dad - dy felt _____ in your jet - black sus-pend-er belt. __

Is it you __ a-gain, __ com-in' 'round __ for more? __
Sev-en-teen __ years old, __ he's touch-in' six - ty - four. __

*See top of first page of song for chord diagrams pertaining to rhythm slashes.

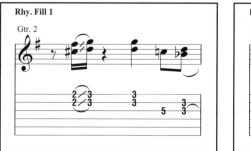

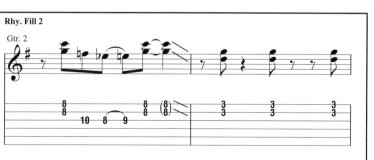

*Substitute G6 chord for A5 chord when recalled as Rhy. Fig. 2.

Verse

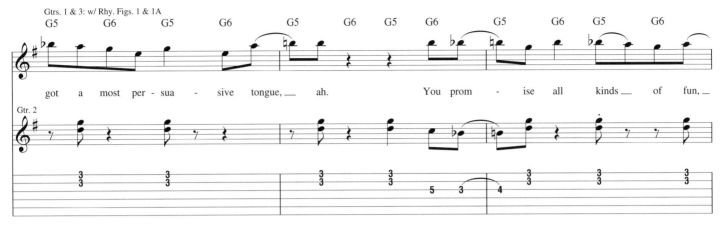

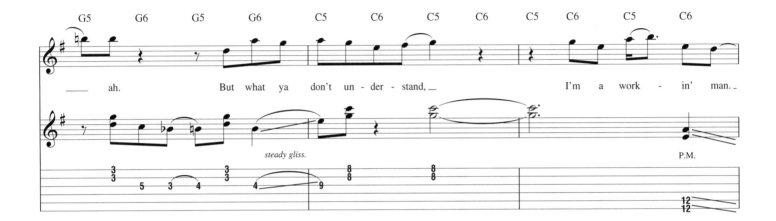

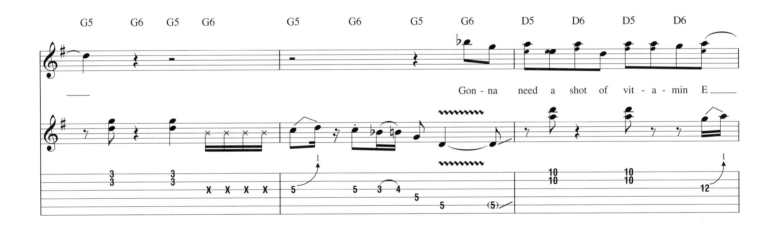

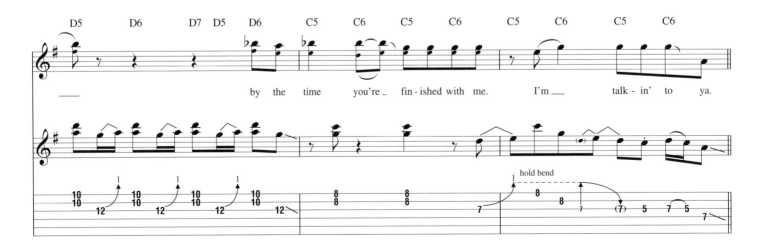

Guitar Solo

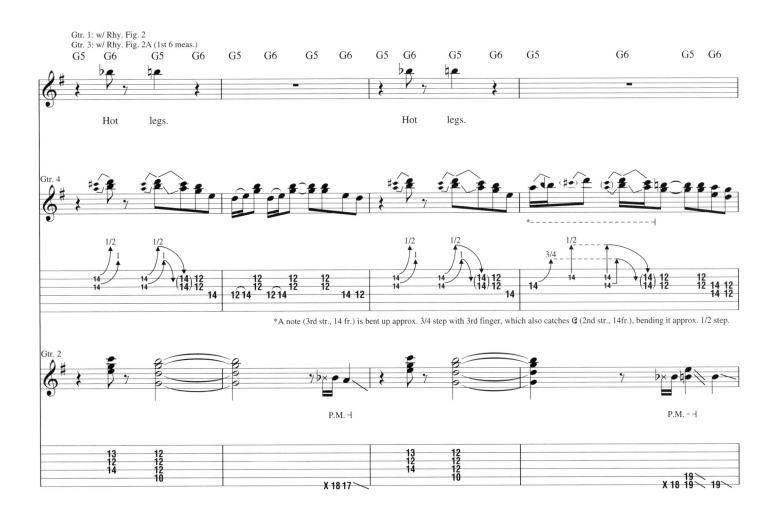

*A note (3rd str., 14 fr.) is bent up approx. 3/4 step with 3rd finger, which also catches G♯ (2nd str., 14fr.), bending it approx. 1/2 step.

D.S. al Coda

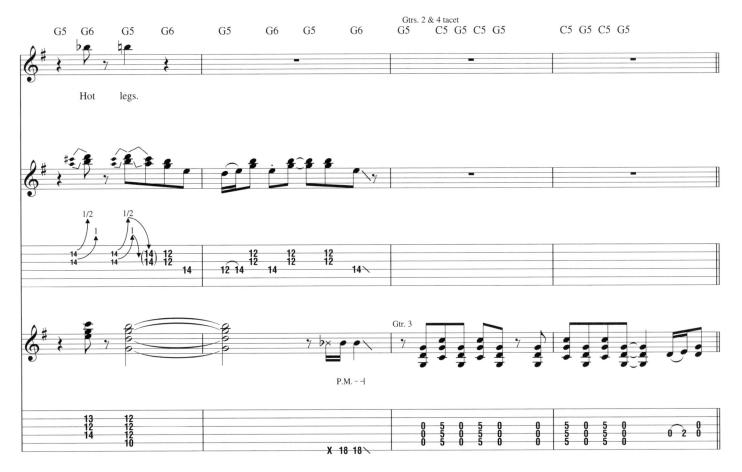

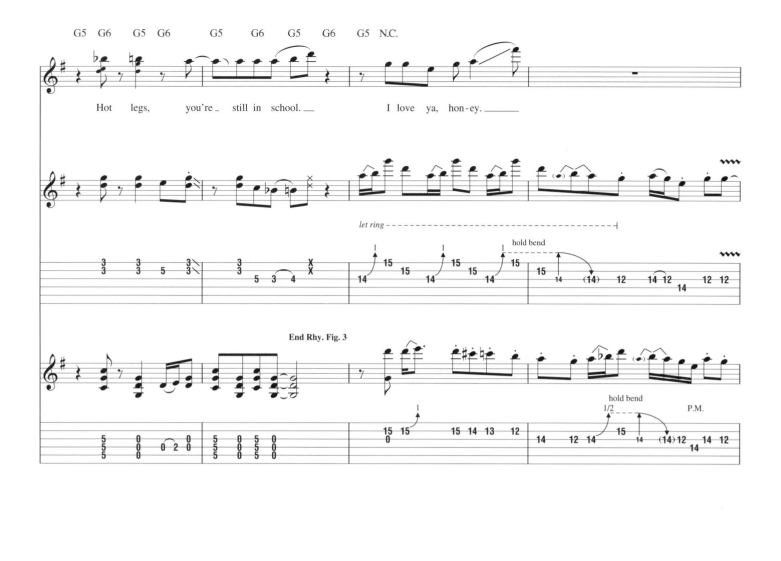

Maggie May

Words and Music by Rod Stewart and Martin Quittenton

Intro
Moderately ♩ = 130

*Two gtrs. (one is a 12-str.) arr. for one.

𝄋 Verse

4th time, Gtr. 3 tacet

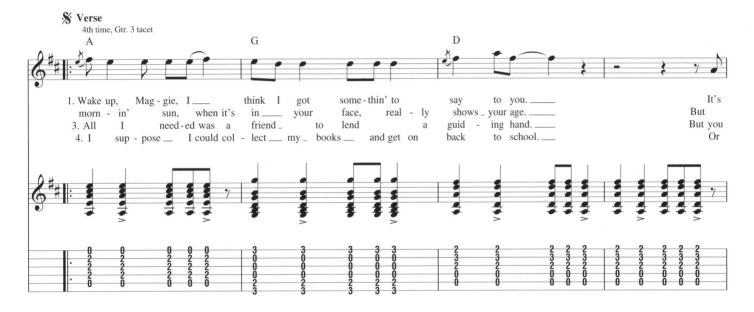

1. Wake up, Mag-gie, I ___ think I got some-thin' to say to you. ___ It's
   morn-in' sun, when it's in ___ your face, real-ly shows ___ your age. ___ But
3. All I need-ed was a friend ___ to lend a guid-ing hand. ___ But you
4. I sup-pose ___ I could col-lect ___ my ___ books ___ and get on back to school. ___ Or

late Sep-tem-ber and I ___ real-ly should ___ be back ___ at school. I
that don't wor-ry me none, ___ in my eyes, ___ you're ev-'ry-thing. ___ I
turned in-to a lov-er and, moth-er, what a lov-er, you wore ___ me ___ out. ___ All ___
steal my Dad-dy's cue ___ and make a liv-ing out of play-in' pool. ___ Or

know I keep you a‑mused, but I feel I'm be ‑ ing used. Oh,
laughed at all of your jokes. My love, you did ‑ n't need to coax. Oh,
 you did was wreck my bed and, in the morn ‑ in', kicked me in the head. Oh,
find my‑self a rock and roll band that needs a help ‑ in' hand. Oh,

4th time, Gtr. 2: w/ Rhy. Fill 4

2nd time, Gtr. 2: w/ Rhy. Fill 1
3rd time, Gtr. 2: w/ Rhy. Fill 3

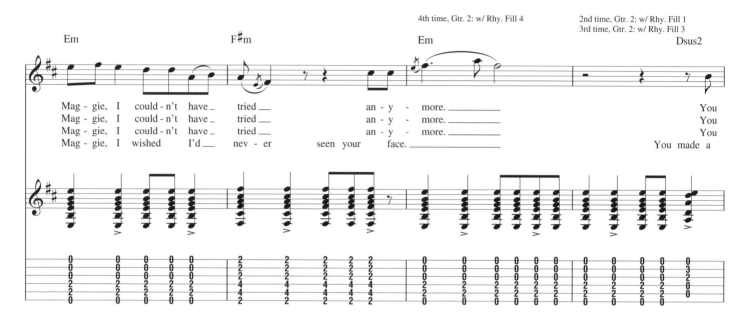

Mag ‑ gie, I could ‑ n't have tried an ‑ y ‑ more. You
Mag ‑ gie, I could ‑ n't have tried an ‑ y ‑ more. You
Mag ‑ gie, I could ‑ n't have tried an ‑ y ‑ more. You
Mag ‑ gie, I wished I'd nev ‑ er seen your face. You made a

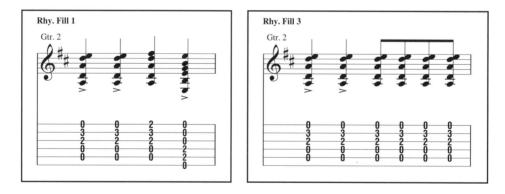

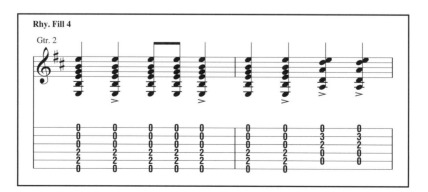

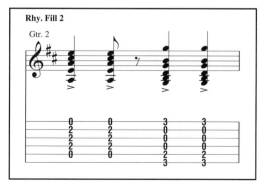

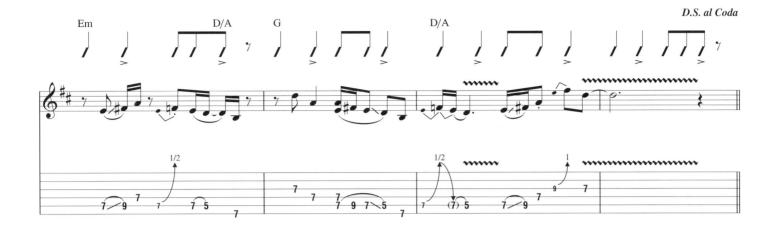

Coda

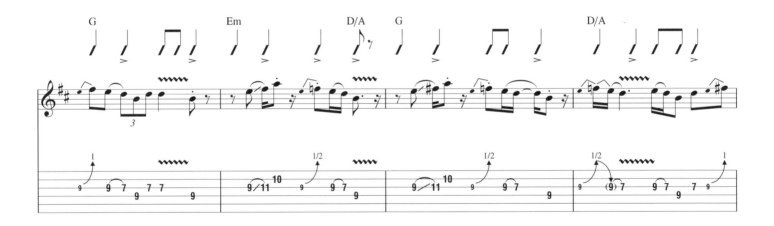

*Two mandolins arr. for gtr. Capoed fret is "0" in tab.

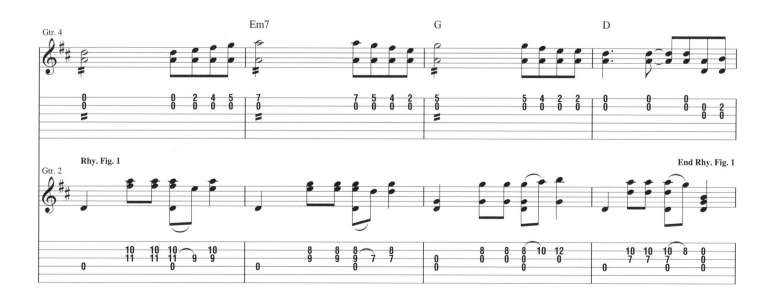

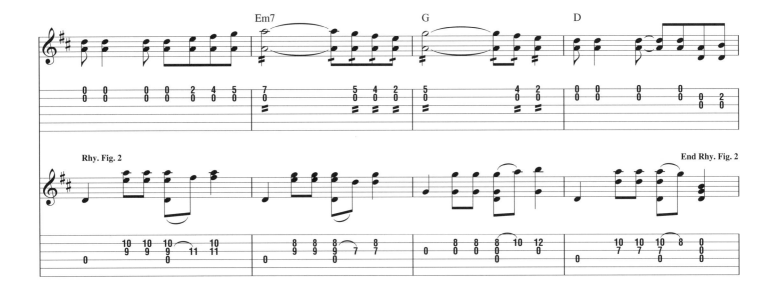

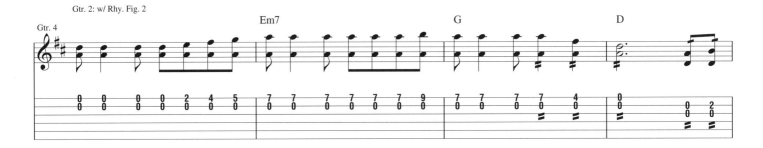

Gtr. 2: w/ Rhy. Fig. 1 (till fade)

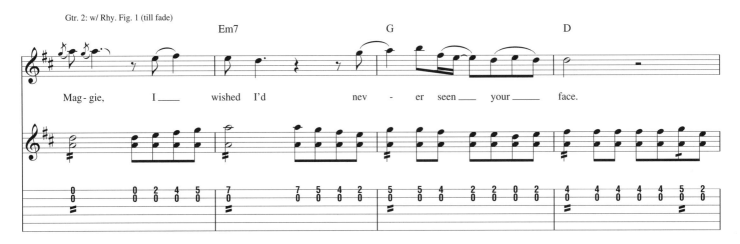

Mag - gie, I ___ wished I'd nev - er seen ___ your ___ face.

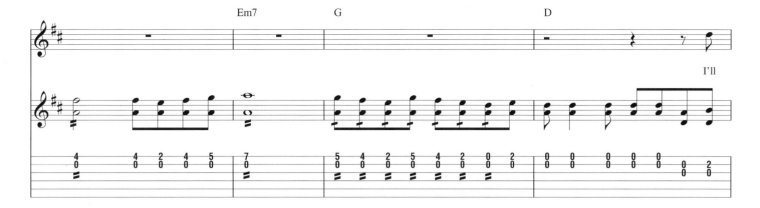

I'll

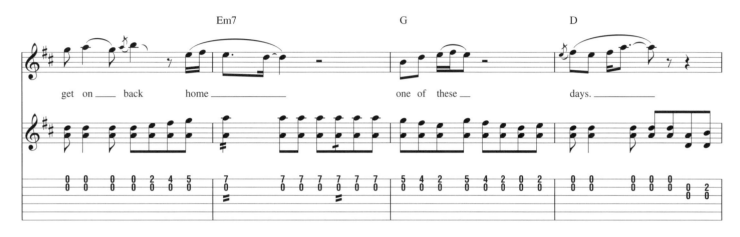

get on ____ back   home _____   one of these ___   days. _____

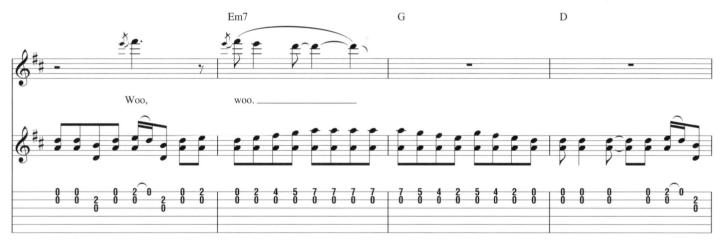

Woo,   woo. _____

Begin fade

Fade out

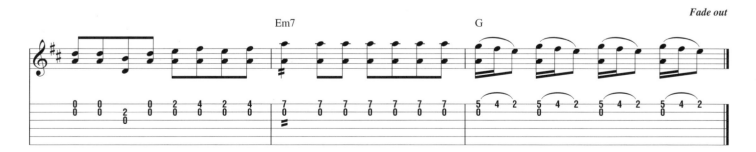

from *Every Picture Tells a Story*
Mandolin Wind
Words and Music by Rod Stewart

Gtr. 1: Capo II
Gtr. 3: Open C tuning:
(low to high) E-C-E-G-C-E
Gtr. 4: Open E tuning:
(low to high) E-B-E-G♯-B-E

*Pedal steel arr. for gtr.

***T = Thumb on 6th string

**Symbols in parentheses represent chord names respective to capoed guitar.
Symbols above reflect actual sounding chords. Capoed fret is "0" in tab.

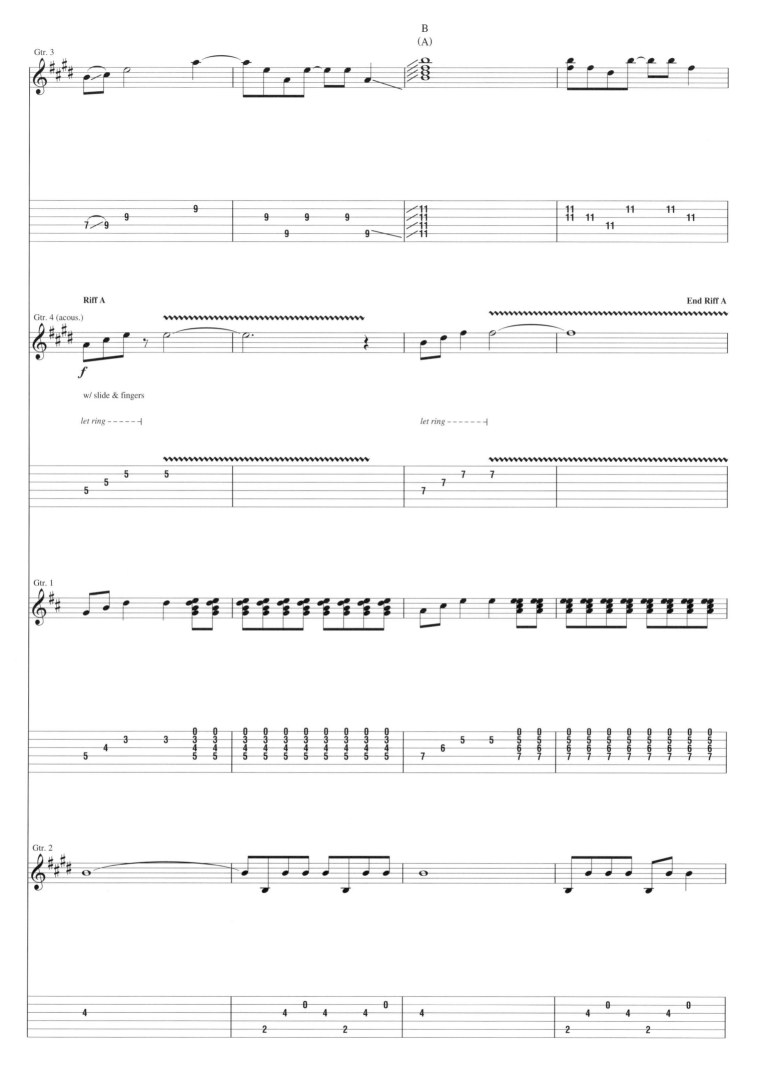

*Slide positioned halfway between the 10th & 11th frets.

rain ___ came, ___ I thought ___ you'd leave. 'Cause I

knew how _ much   you love _ the sun.   But you

love __ ya.

Verse

snow ___ fell ___ with-out ___ a break. ___

Buf-fa-lo died in the fro-zen fields, you know. ___ Through the

next few lines come rea - lly hard.

Don't have much, but what I've got is yours. Ex -

Chorus

Gtr. 1: w/ Rhy. Fig. 3 (1st 6 meas.)

Outro

Reason to Believe

Words and Music by Tim Hardin

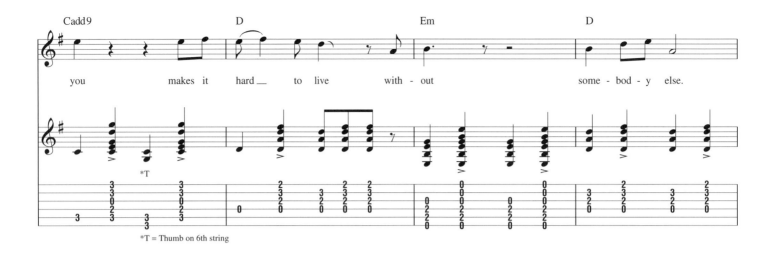

Verse

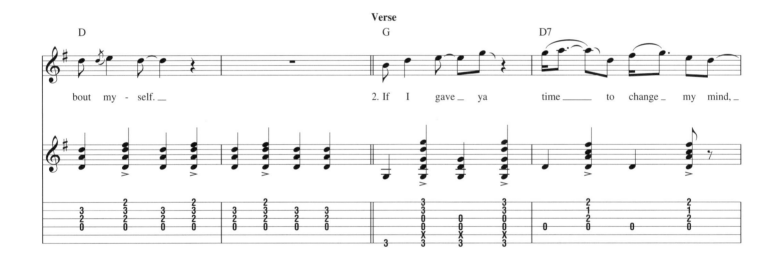

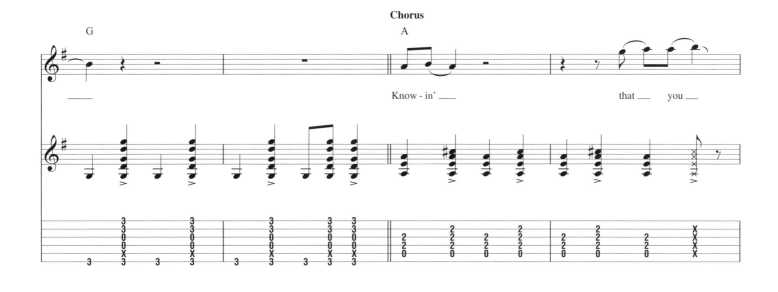

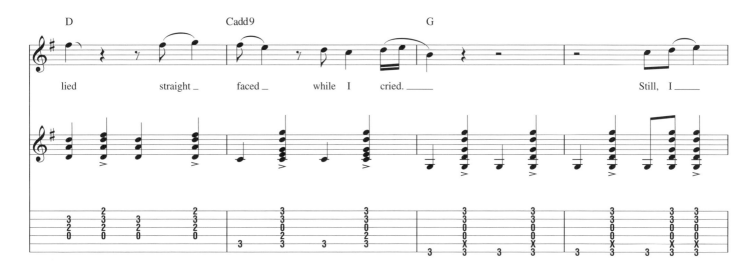

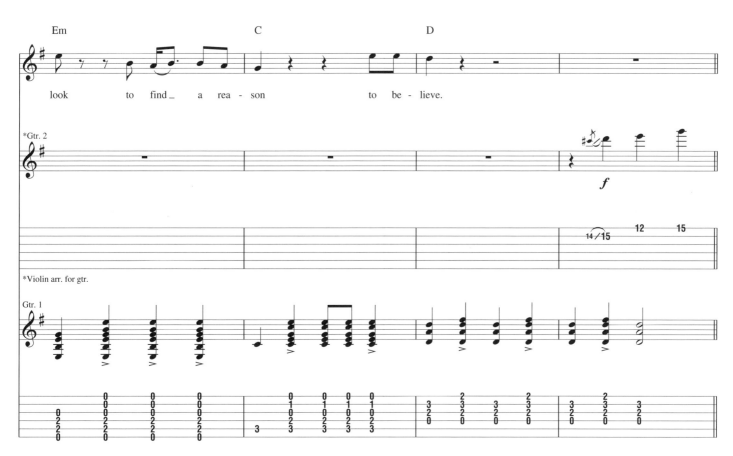

Violin Solo

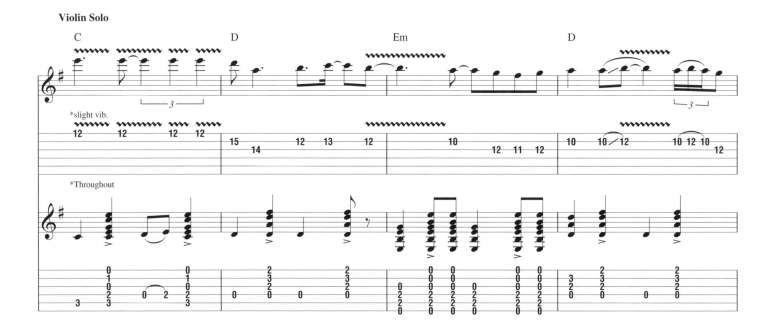

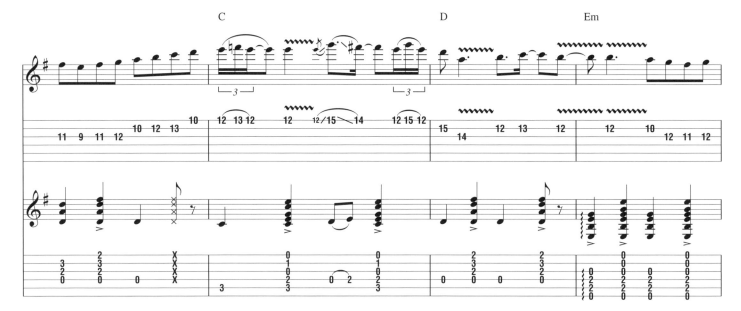

Verse

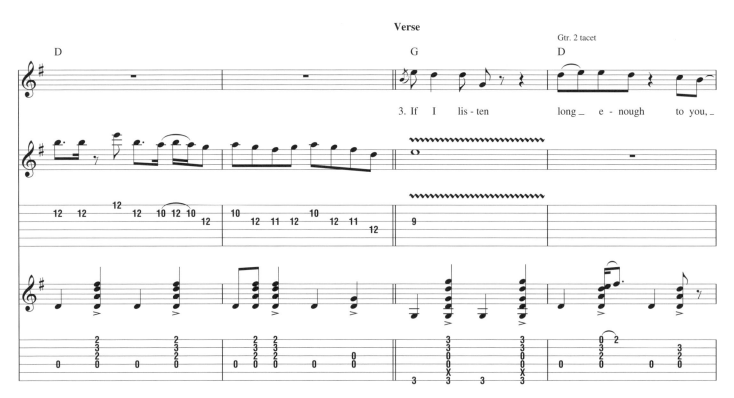

I'd find ___ a way ___ to be - lieve ___ that it's ___ all ___

Gtr. 1

Chorus

true. Know - in' ___ that ___ you ___

lied ___ straight ___ faced ___ while I cried. ___ Still, I

look to find ___ a rea - son to be - lieve.

Free time

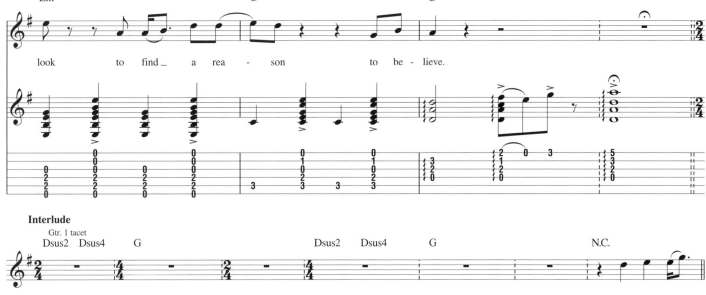

Interlude

Gtr. 1 tacet

Dsus2 Dsus4 G   Dsus2 Dsus4 G   N.C.

Some - one like ___

*See top of first page of song for chord diagrams pertaining to rhythm slashes.

bout my - self. _ Someone _____ like _ you makes it hard to live with - out

Outro
Begin fade

some - bod - y else.

Fade out

Stay with Me

Words and Music by Rod Stewart and Ron Wood

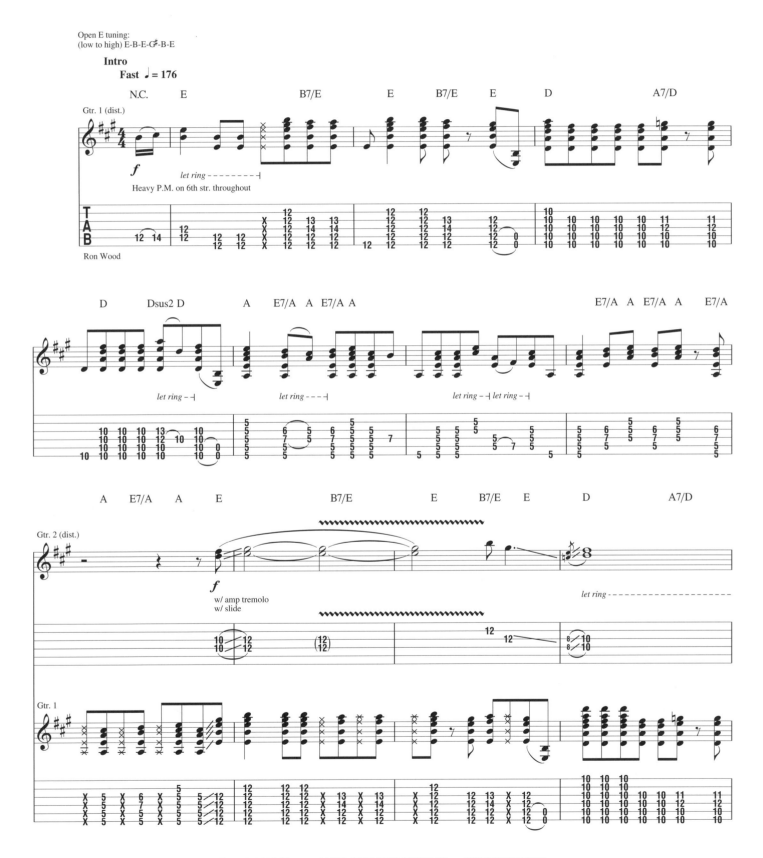

*T = Thumb on 6th string

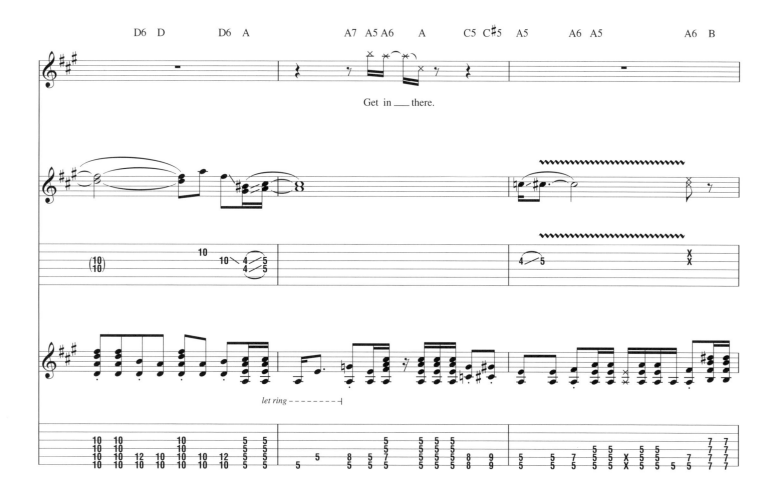

Get in ___ there.

*1. In the morn -

*Rod Stewart

137

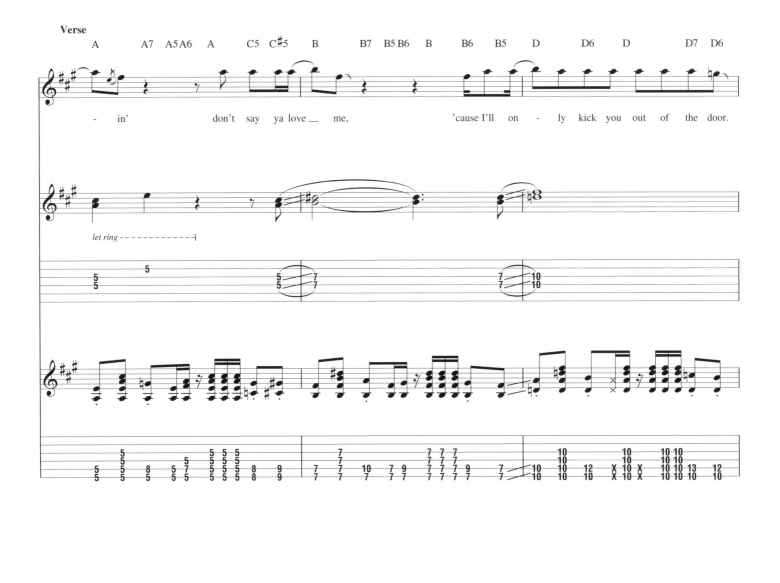

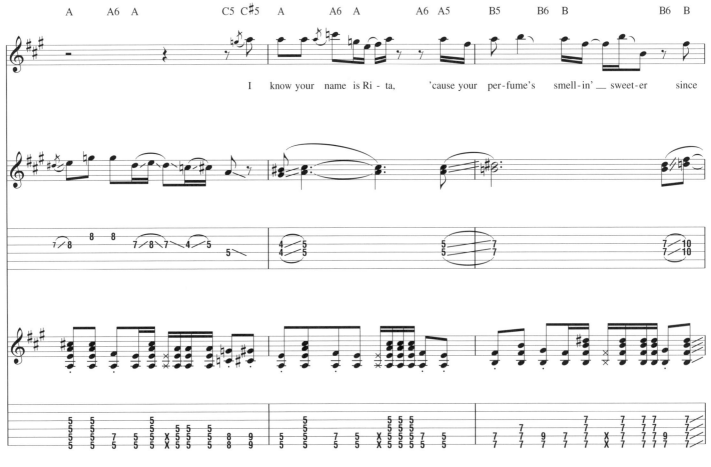

Verse
A A7 A5 A6 A C5 C#5 B B7 B5 B6 B B6 B5 D D6 D D7 D6
- in' don't say ya love __ me, 'cause I'll on - ly kick you out of the door.
let ring
A A6 A C5 C#5 A A6 A A6 A5 B5 B6 B B6 B
I know your name is Ri - ta, 'cause your per-fume's smell-in' __ sweet-er since

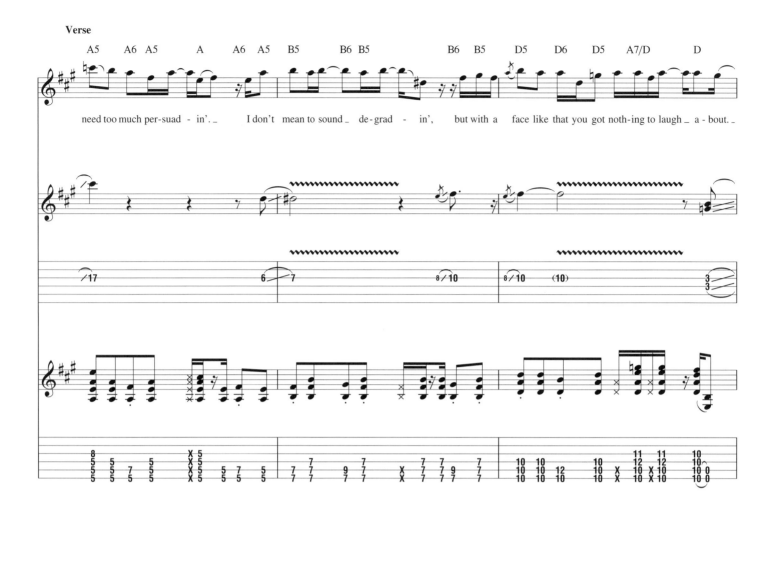

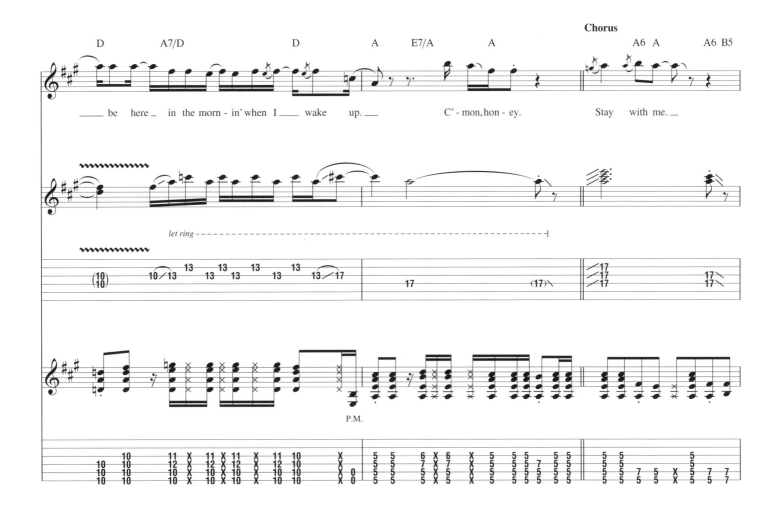

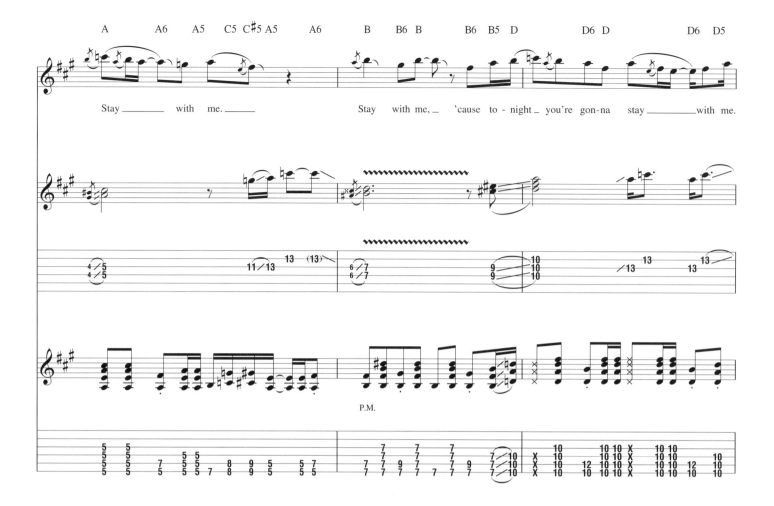

Stay _____ with me. _____ Stay with me, _ 'cause to - night _ you're gon-na stay _____ with me.

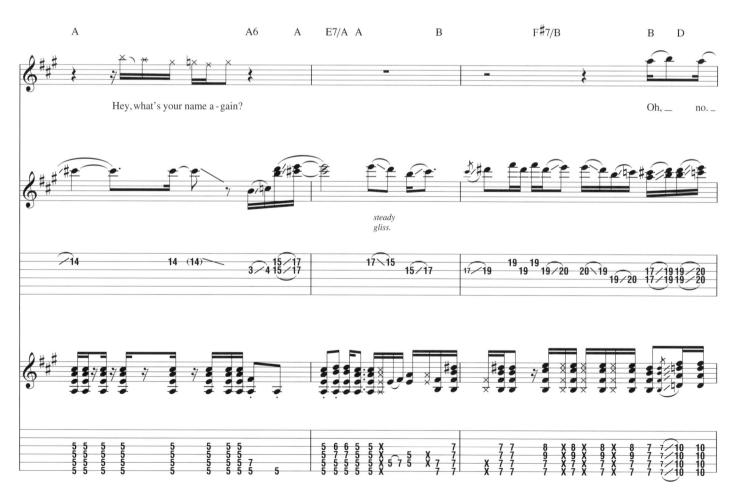

Hey, what's your name a - gain? Oh, _ no. _

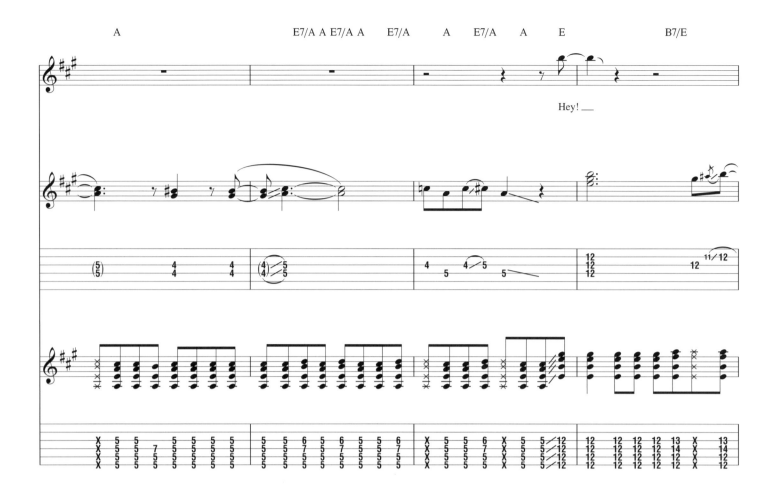

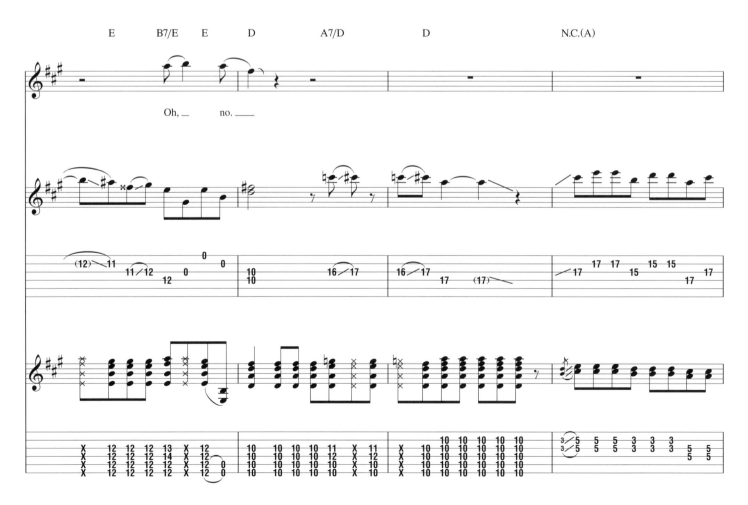

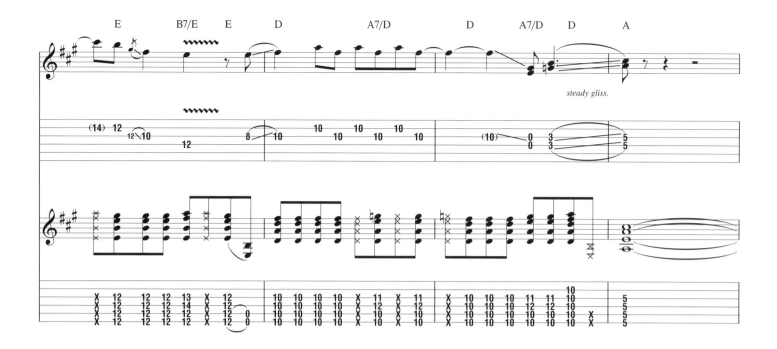

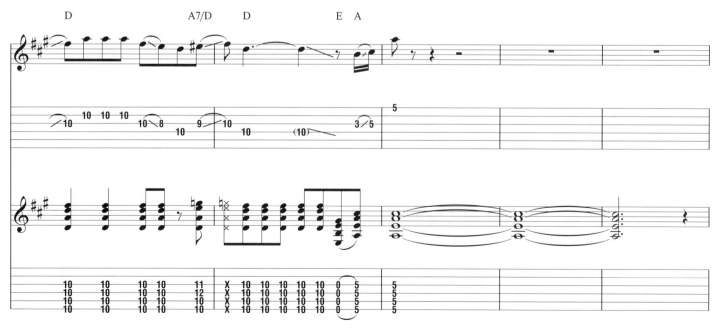

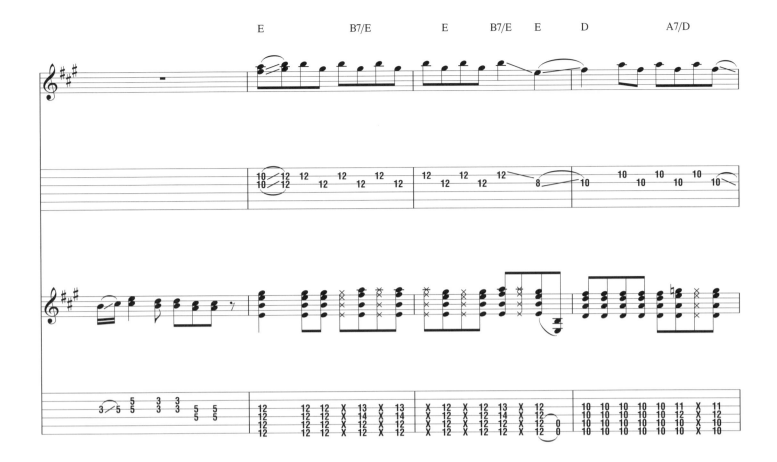

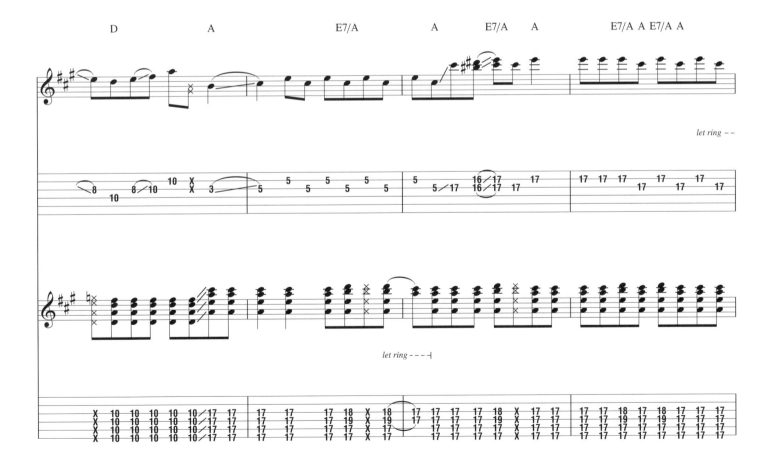

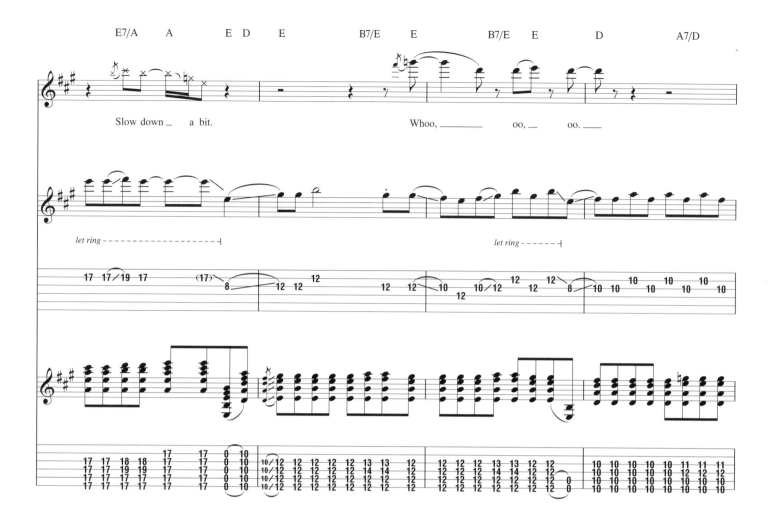

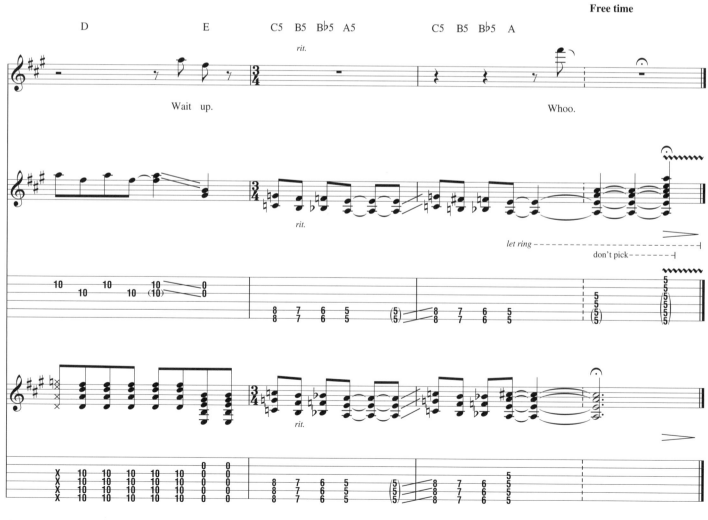

from *A Night on the Town*

Tonight's the Night (Gonna Be Alright)

Words and Music by Rod Stewart

*Chord symbols reflect overall harmony.

Re - lax, ba - by, and draw that __ blind. __

*T = Thumb on 6th string

Verse

2. Kick off your shoes __ and sit right __ down. __ Loos - en up that __ pret - ty French __ gown.

love ya, girl, __ ain't no - bod-y gon - na stop us now. __

Verse

3. Come on, an - gel, my heart's on fire. __ Don't de - ny __ your man's de - sire. __

You'd be a fool _ to stop this _ tide. _ Spread your wings and let me come in - side. _ 'Cause _

Chorus

to - night's _ the night, _ it's gon-na be _ al - right 'cause I ___

slight vib.

1 hold bend

1 hold bend

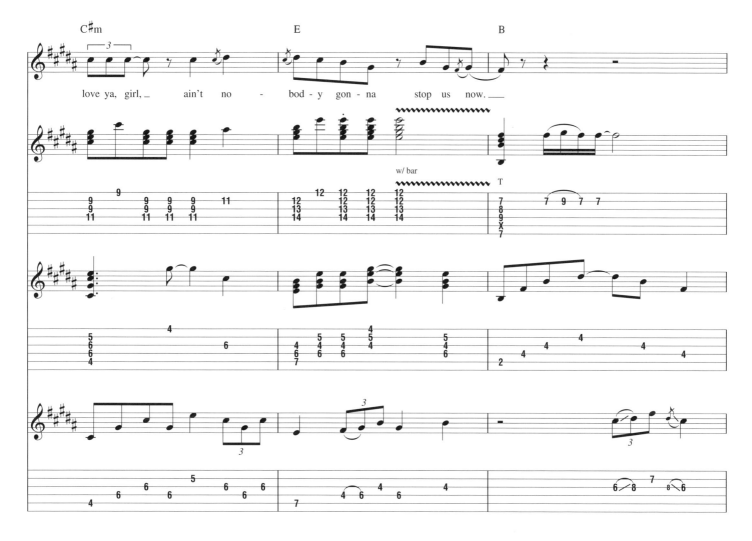

love ya, girl,___ ain't no - bod - y gon - na stop us now.___

Saxophone Solo

**Bends at 9th fret, 3rd string are played with index finger (next 8 meas.).

***Composite arrangement

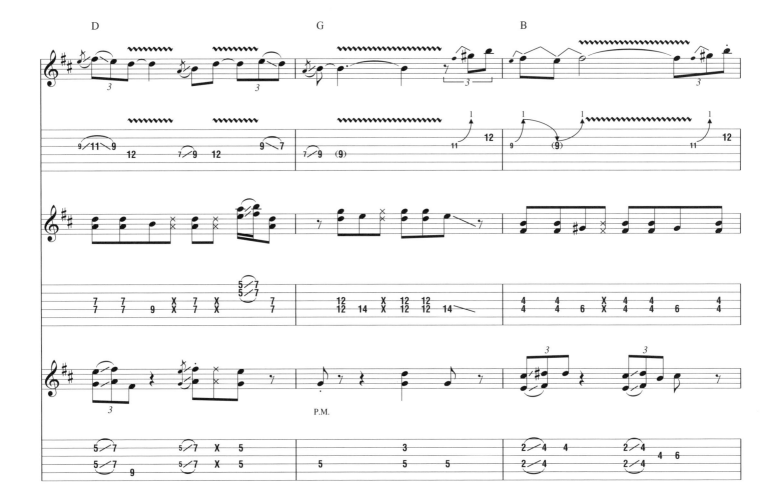

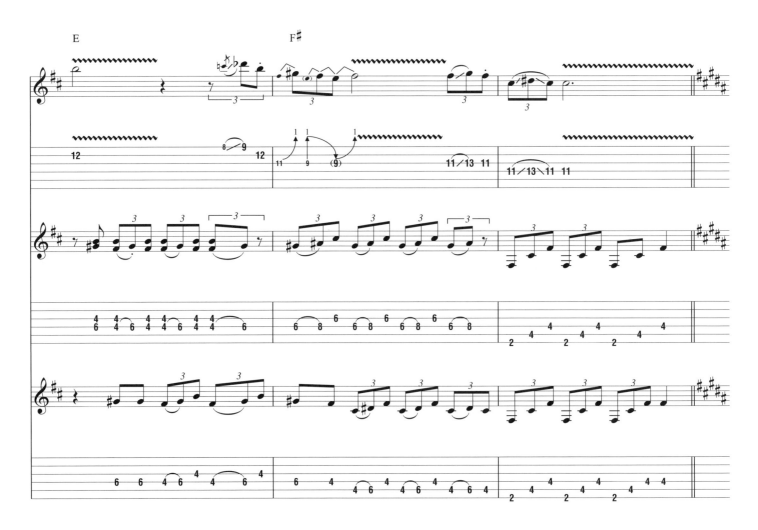

4. Don't say a word, my vir-gin child. __ Just __ let your in-hib-i-tions run wild. __

The se-cret is a-bout to un-fold __ up-stairs, __ be-fore the night's too old. __

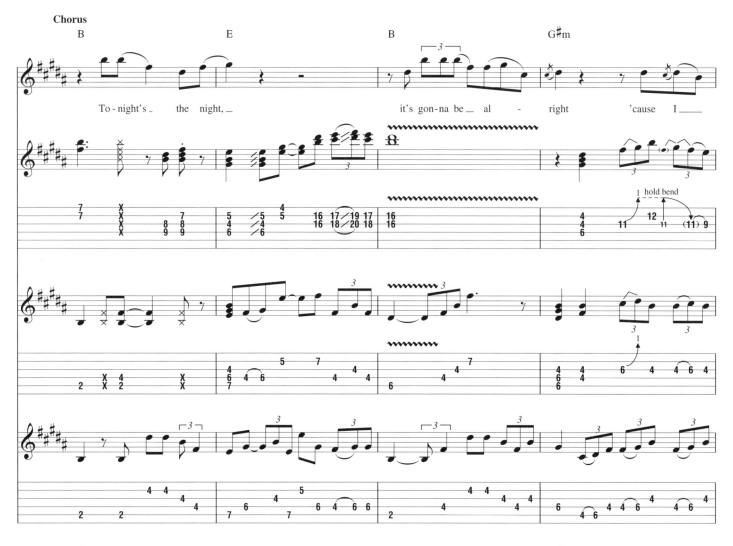

To-night's _ the night, _ it's gon-na be _ al - right 'cause I _

love ya, girl, _ ain't no - bod-y gon-na stop us now. _

Woo.

Outro

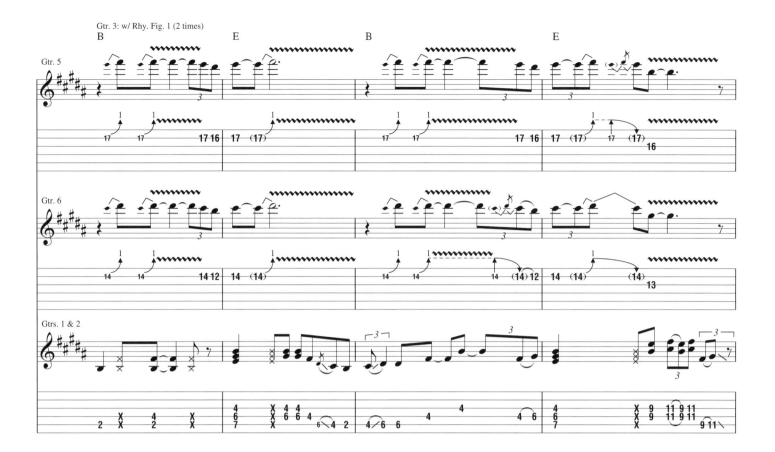

from *Never a Dull Moment*

You Wear It Well

Words and Music by Rod Stewart and Martin Quittenton

*Chord symbols reflect implied harmony.

**Pluck chord w/ pick and fingers.

***slight vib.

***Throughout

†T = Thumb on 6th string

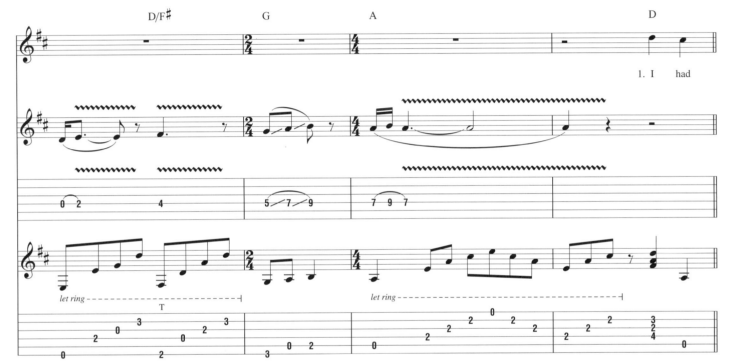

Verse

noth-ing to do ___ on this hot af-ter-noon ___ but to set-tle down and write you a line. ___ I been

meaning to phone ___ ya, but from Min-ne-so-ta, hell, ___ it's been a ver-y long time. You wear ___ it well.___

Chorus

A lit-tle old fash-ioned, but that's ___ al-right.___ 2. Well, I sup-

Chorus

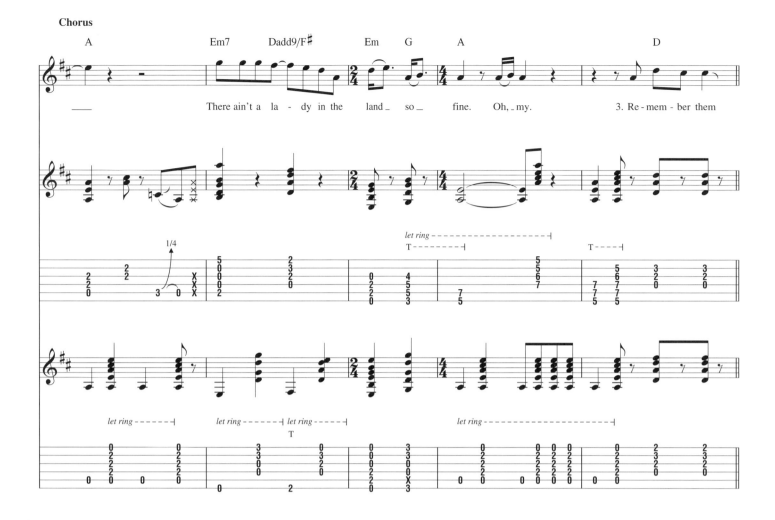

There ain't a la - dy in the land so fine. Oh, my. 3. Re - mem - ber them

Verse

base - ment par - ties, your broth-er's ka - ra - te, the all day rock -'n'- roll shows? Them

home - sick blues _ and the rad - i - cal views _ have-n't left a mark _ on _ you. You wear _ it

Chorus

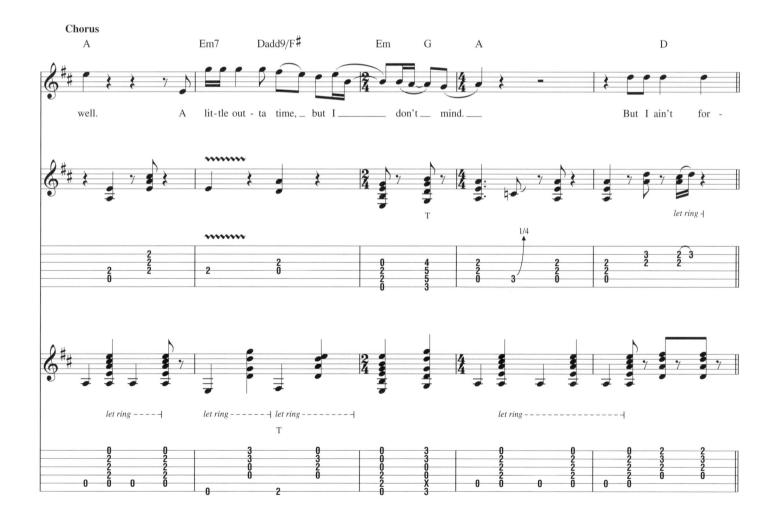

well. A lit-tle out-a time, _ but I _ don't _ mind. _ But I ain't for -

Violin Solo

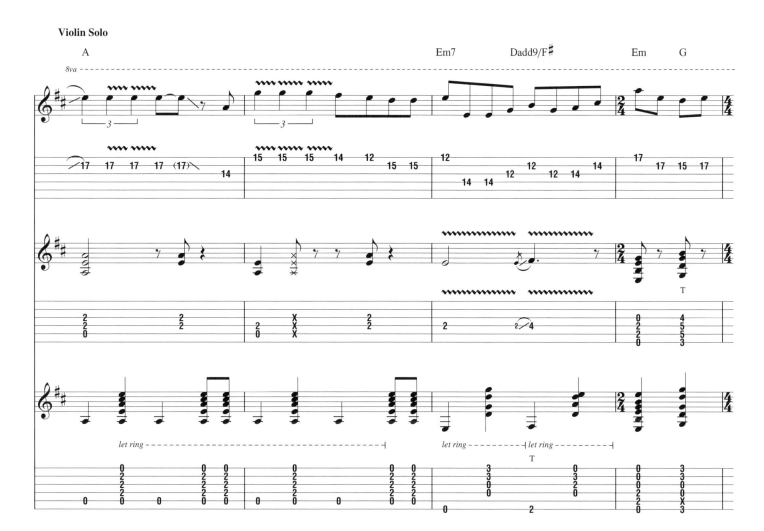

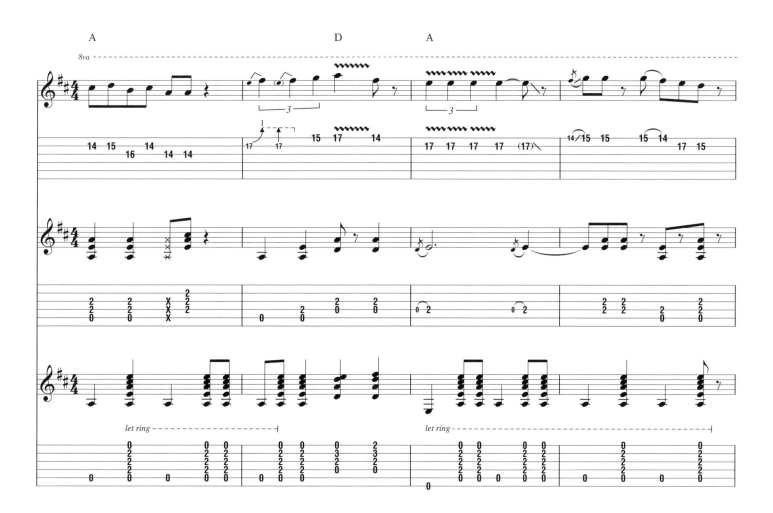

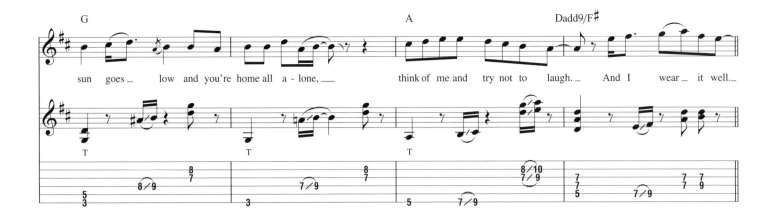

sun goes_ low and you're home all a-lone,_ think of me and try not to laugh._ And I wear_ it well._

Chorus

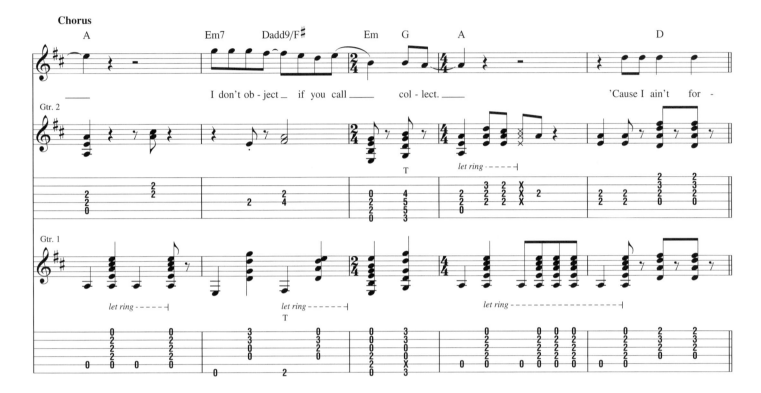

I don't ob-ject_ if you call_ col-lect._ 'Cause I ain't for-

Bridge

get-tin' that you_ were once mine. But I blew_ it with-out e-ven try-in'. Now I'm

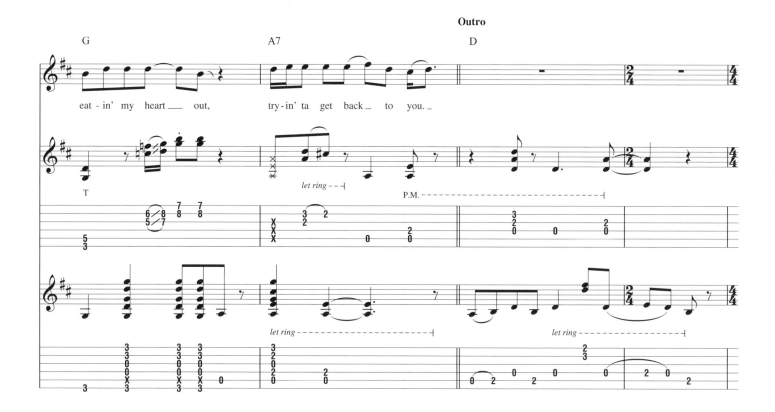

eat - in' my heart ___ out,   try - in' ta get back _ to you. _

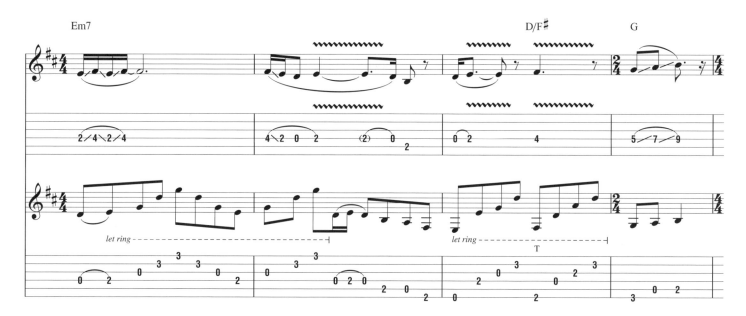

After all this, __ hope it's the same __ ad-dress. __

Begin fade

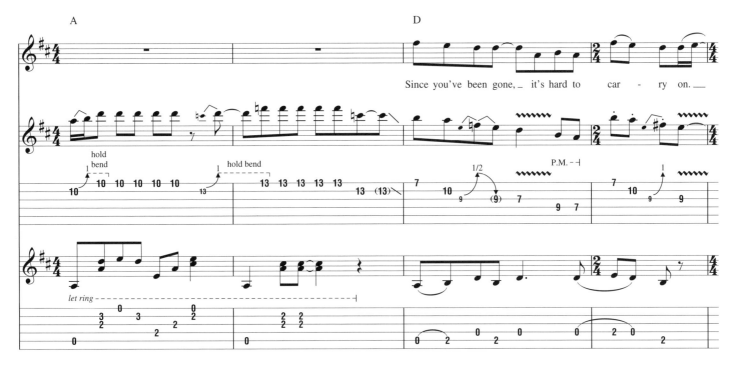

Since you've been gone, __ it's hard to car - ry on. __

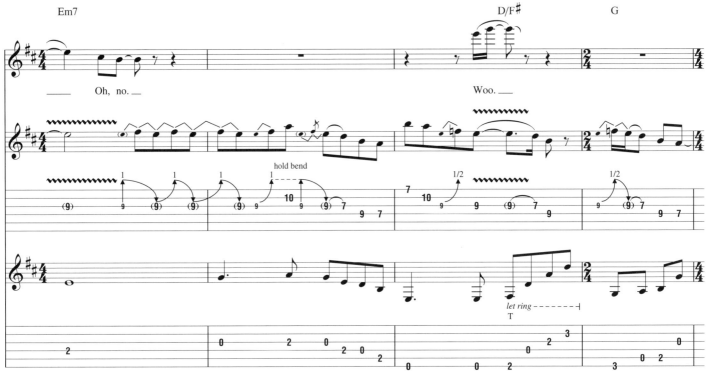

Oh, no. __

Woo. __

Fade out

from *Foot Loose and Fancy Free*

You're in My Heart

Words and Music by Rod Stewart

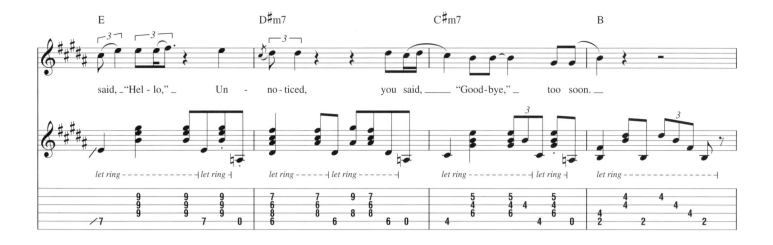

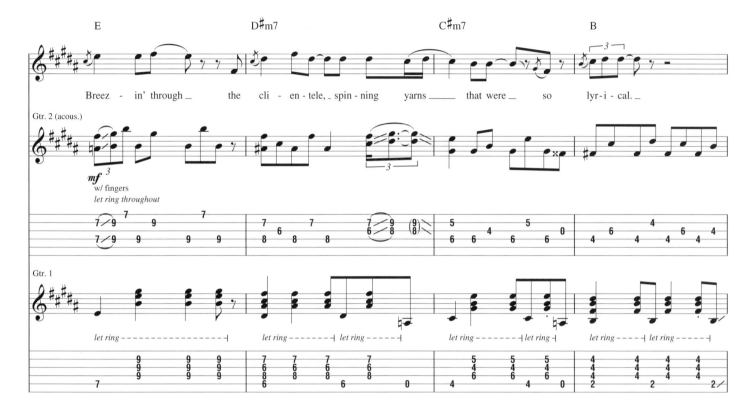

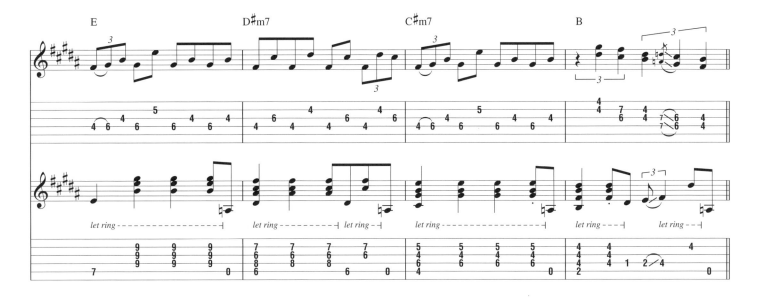

Verse

2. I took all __ those hab-its of yours __ that, in the be - gin-ning, were __ hard to ac - cept. __ Your

fash - ion sense, __ beards - ly prints, __ I put down to ex - pe - ri - ence. __ The

big bos-omed la-dy with a Dutch ac-cent __ who tried to change __ my point of view. ___ Her

(Oo. _____

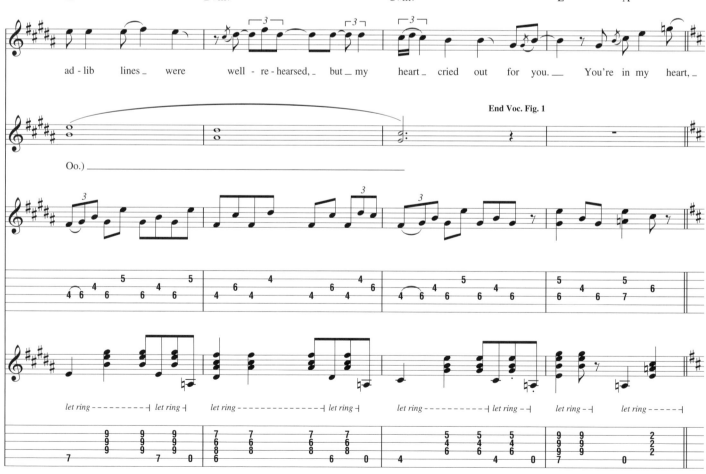

ad-lib lines __ were well-re-hearsed, __ but __ my heart __ cried out for you. __ You're in my heart, __

Oo.) _____

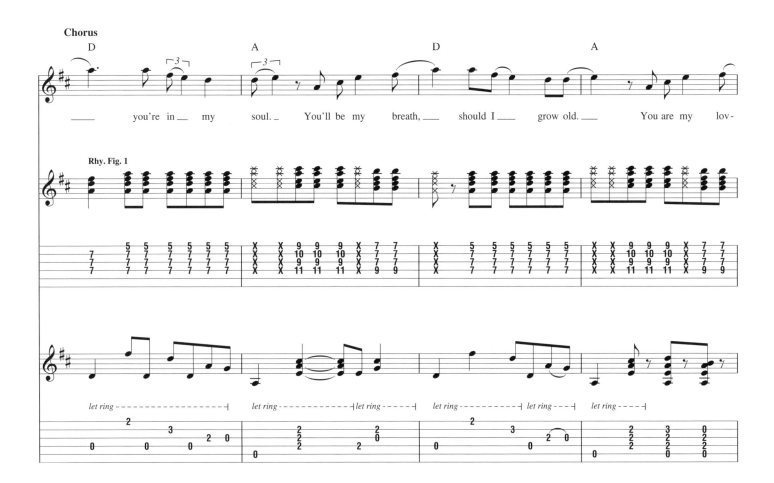

you're in my soul. You'll be my breath, should I grow old. You are my lov-

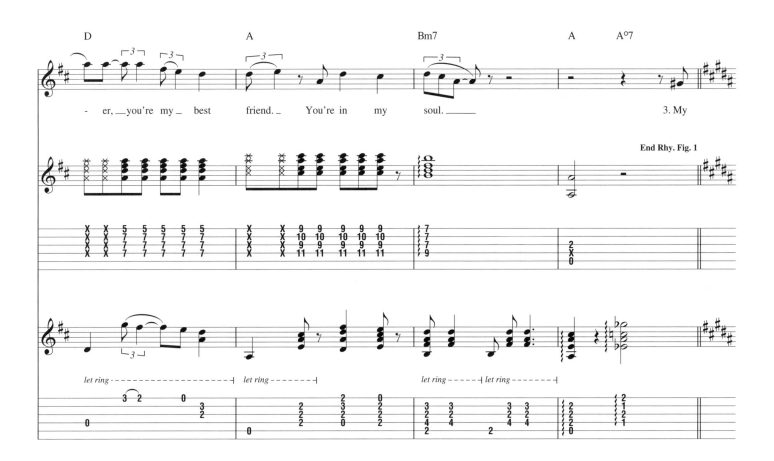

- er, you're my best friend. You're in my soul. 3. My

Verse

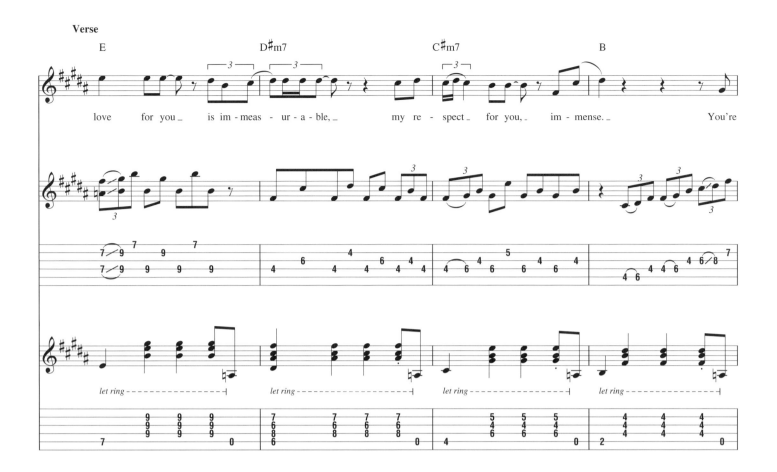

love for you _ is im-meas-ur-a-ble, _ my re-spect _ for you, _ im-mense. _ You're

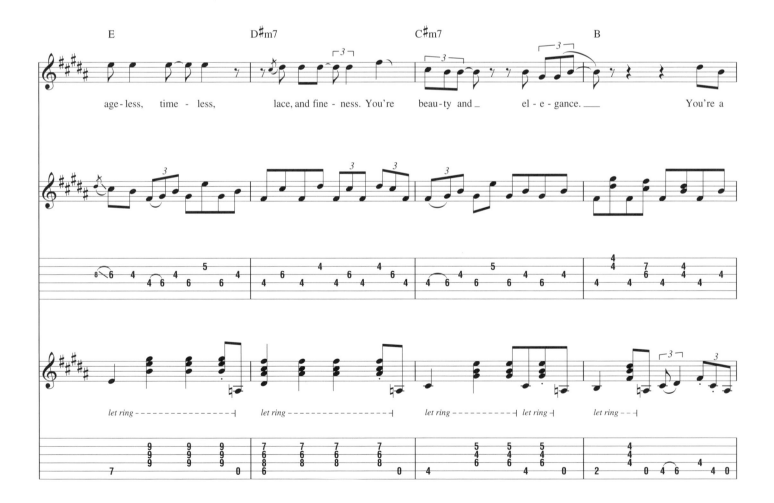

age-less, time-less, lace, and fine-ness. You're beau-ty and _ el-e-gance. ___ You're a

*Sung as even eighth-notes.

Gtr. 2: w/ Rhy. Fig. 2

-er, you're my best friend. You're in my soul. Oh, yeah. You're in my

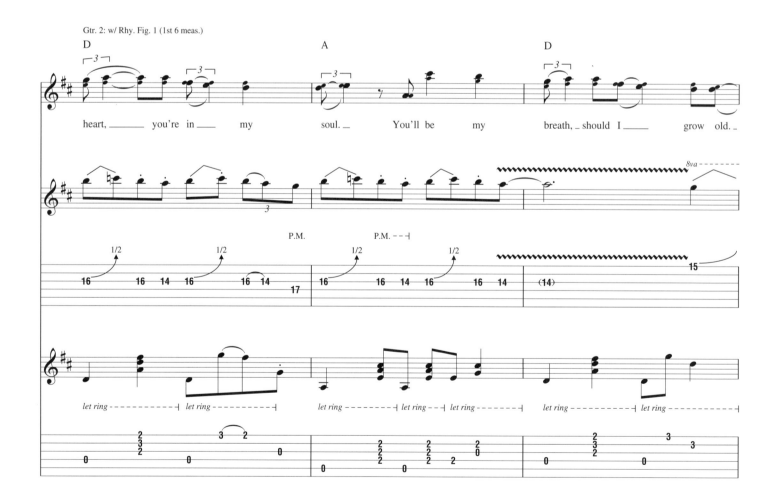

Gtr. 2: w/ Rhy. Fig. 1 (1st 6 meas.)

heart, you're in my soul. You'll be my breath, should I grow old.

You are my lov - er, you're my ___ best friend. You're in ___ my

soul.

Free Time

Begin fade

Fade out

193

from *Tonight I'm Yours*

Young Turks

Words and Music by Rod Stewart, Kevin Savigar, Carmine Appice and Duane Hitchings

*Two gtrs. arr. for one.

**Chord symbols reflect overall harmony.

***Bass plays B♭.

†Kybds. arr. for gtr.

††See top of page for chord diagrams pertaining to rhythm slashes.

†††Set for one octave above.

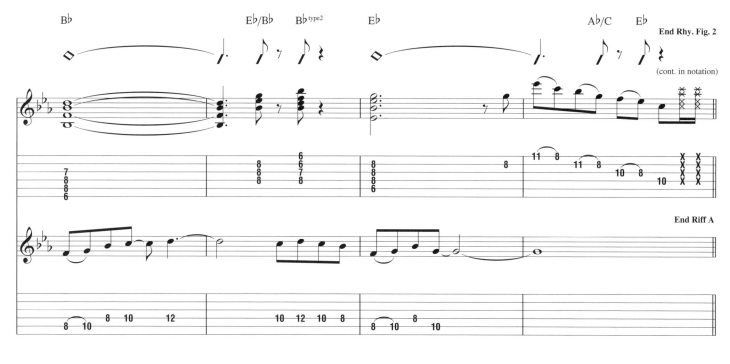

Verse

1. Bil - ly left his home with a dol - lar in his pock - et and a head-full of dreams. __ He said,

"Some - how, some way it's got - ta get bet - ter than this." __

life is so brief ___ and time is a thief ___ when you're un-de-cid-ed. ___ And like a

fist - ful of sand, it can slip right through your hands. ___ Young

Gtr. 2

Gtr. 1 Rhy. Fig. 4   End Rhy. Fig. 4

P.M. ----------

𝄋 **Chorus**

Gtr. 2 tacet

hearts   be   free   to - night, ___

Voc. Fig. 1

(Hearts   be   free   to - night, ___

Riff B
Gtr. 4 (clean)

mf
w/ chorus
let ring throughout

Gtr. 1 Rhy. Fig. 5   End Rhy. Fig. 5

P.M. --

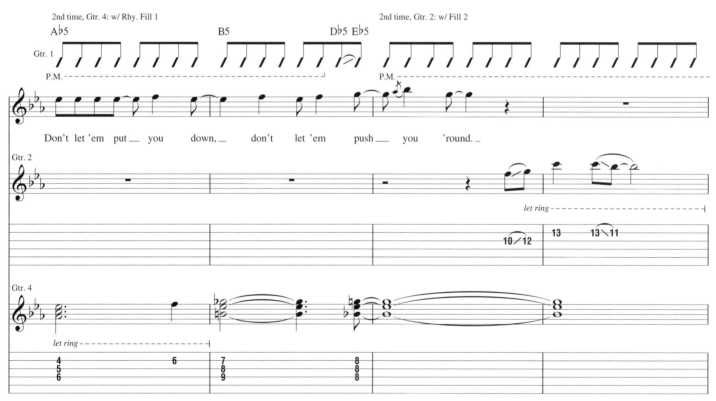

Hap - pi - ness was found in each oth - er's arms, ___ as ex - pect - ed. Yeah. ___

Gtr. 1: w/ Rhy. Fig. 4

D.S. al Coda

Bil - ly pierced his ears, drove a pick-up like a lun - a - tic. ___ Woo. ___ Young

let ring - - - - - - - - - - - - - - -

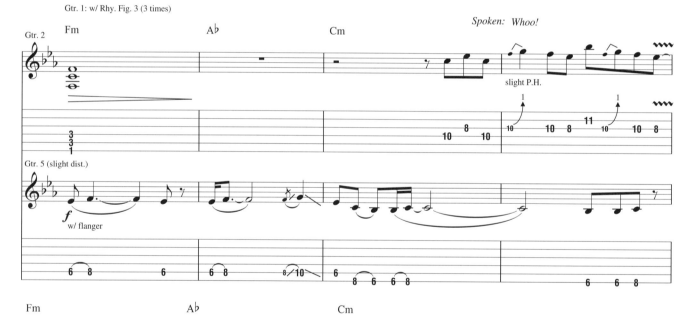

Coda

Guitar Solo

Gtr. 1: w/ Rhy. Fig. 3 (3 times)

Spoken: Whoo!

Gtr. 2

slight P.H.

Gtr. 5 (slight dist.)

f w/ flanger

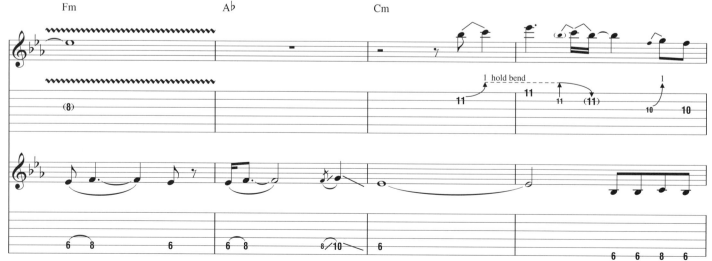

1 hold bend

both real __ sor-ry that it had to turn out __ this __ way, but there

ain't no point in talk - in' when there's no - bod - y lis' - t'nin', so we just ran a - way.

Gtr. 1: w/ Rhy. Fig. 4

Pat - ty gave birth to a ten pound ba - by boy." __ Yeah! __ Young

Outro-Chorus

Bkgd. Voc.: w/ Voc. Fig. 1 (5 times)
Gtr. 1: w/ Rhy. Fig. 6 (till fade)
Gtr. 4: w/ Riff B (last 4 meas., till fade)
Gtr. 2 tacet

Play 3 times

hearts be free to - night, __ time is on __ your side. __ Young

hearts got - ta run free, be free, live free, time is on your, time __ is on your side.
hearts, be free __ to - night, to - night, to - night, __ to - night, to - night. Yeah.

Time, __ time, __ time, __ time is on your side, is on your side, is on your side. Young
Oo. __ Oo. __ Oo. __

Play 4 times and fade

GUITAR NOTATION LEGEND

Guitar music can be notated three different ways: on a *musical staff*, in *tablature*, and in *rhythm slashes*.

RHYTHM SLASHES are written above the staff. Strum chords in the rhythm indicated. Use the chord diagrams found at the top of the first page of the transcription for the appropriate chord voicings. Round noteheads indicate single notes.

THE MUSICAL STAFF shows pitches and rhythms and is divided by bar lines into measures. Pitches are named after the first seven letters of the alphabet.

TABLATURE graphically represents the guitar fingerboard. Each horizontal line represents a string, and each number represents a fret.

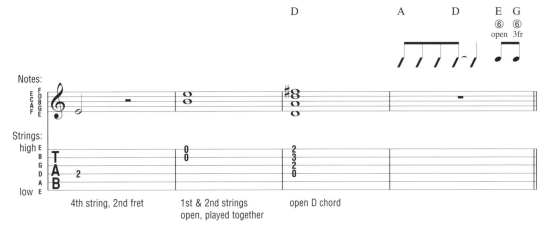

4th string, 2nd fret   1st & 2nd strings open, played together   open D chord

Definitions for Special Guitar Notation

HALF-STEP BEND: Strike the note and bend up 1/2 step.

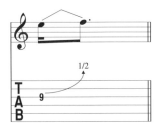

WHOLE-STEP BEND: Strike the note and bend up one step.

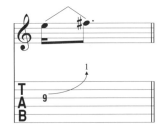

GRACE NOTE BEND: Strike the note and immediately bend up as indicated.

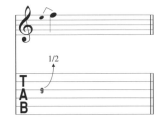

SLIGHT (MICROTONE) BEND: Strike the note and bend up 1/4 step.

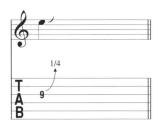

BEND AND RELEASE: Strike the note and bend up as indicated, then release back to the original note. Only the first note is struck.

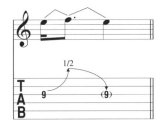

PRE-BEND: Bend the note as indicated, then strike it.

PRE-BEND AND RELEASE: Bend the note as indicated. Strike it and release the bend back to the original note.

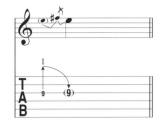

UNISON BEND: Strike the two notes simultaneously and bend the lower note up to the pitch of the higher.

VIBRATO: The string is vibrated by rapidly bending and releasing the note with the fretting hand.

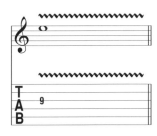

WIDE VIBRATO: The pitch is varied to a greater degree by vibrating with the fretting hand.

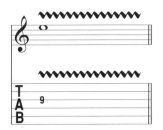

HAMMER-ON: Strike the first (lower) note with one finger, then sound the higher note (on the same string) with another finger by fretting it without picking.

PULL-OFF: Place both fingers on the notes to be sounded. Strike the first note and without picking, pull the finger off to sound the second (lower) note.

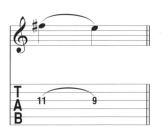

LEGATO SLIDE: Strike the first note and then slide the same fret-hand finger up or down to the second note. The second note is not struck.

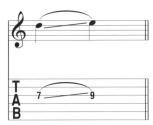

SHIFT SLIDE: Same as legato slide, except the second note is struck.

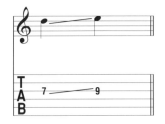

TRILL: Very rapidly alternate between the notes indicated by continuously hammering on and pulling off.

TAPPING: Hammer ("tap") the fret indicated with the pick-hand index or middle finger and pull off to the note fretted by the fret hand.

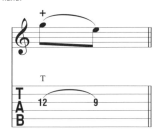

NATURAL HARMONIC: Strike the note while the fret-hand lightly touches the string directly over the fret indicated.

PINCH HARMONIC: The note is fretted normally and a harmonic is produced by adding the edge of the thumb or the tip of the index finger of the pick hand to the normal pick attack.

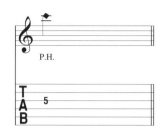

HARP HARMONIC: The note is fretted normally and a harmonic is produced by gently resting the pick hand's index finger directly above the indicated fret (in parentheses) while the pick hand's thumb or pick assists by plucking the appropriate string.

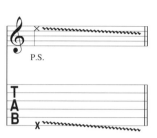

PICK SCRAPE: The edge of the pick is rubbed down (or up) the string, producing a scratchy sound.

MUFFLED STRINGS: A percussive sound is produced by laying the fret hand across the string(s) without depressing, and striking them with the pick hand.

PALM MUTING: The note is partially muted by the pick hand lightly touching the string(s) just before the bridge.

RAKE: Drag the pick across the strings indicated with a single motion.

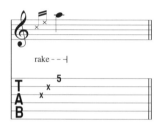

TREMOLO PICKING: The note is picked as rapidly and continuously as possible.

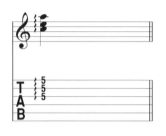

ARPEGGIATE: Play the notes of the chord indicated by quickly rolling them from bottom to top.

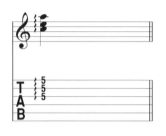

VIBRATO BAR DIVE AND RETURN: The pitch of the note or chord is dropped a specified number of steps (in rhythm), then returned to the original pitch.

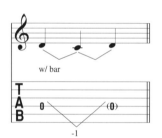

VIBRATO BAR SCOOP: Depress the bar just before striking the note, then quickly release the bar.

VIBRATO BAR DIP: Strike the note and then immediately drop a specified number of steps, then release back to the original pitch.

Additional Musical Definitions

> (accent)	• Accentuate note (play it louder).	
^ (accent)	• Accentuate note with great intensity.	
• (staccato)	• Play the note short.	
⊓	• Downstroke	
V	• Upstroke	
D.S. al Coda	• Go back to the sign (𝄋), then play until the measure marked "*To Coda*," then skip to the section labelled "**Coda**."	
D.C. al Fine	• Go back to the beginning of the song and play until the measure marked "*Fine*" (end).	

Rhy. Fig.
• Label used to recall a recurring accompaniment pattern (usually chordal).

Riff
• Label used to recall composed, melodic lines (usually single notes) which recur.

Fill
• Label used to identify a brief melodic figure which is to be inserted into the arrangement.

Rhy. Fill
• A chordal version of a Fill.

tacet
• Instrument is silent (drops out).

• Repeat measures between signs.

• When a repeated section has different endings, play the first ending only the first time and the second ending only the second time.

NOTE: Tablature numbers in parentheses mean:
    1. The note is being sustained over a system (note in standard notation is tied), or
    2. The note is sustained, but a new articulation (such as a hammer-on, pull-off, slide or vibrato) begins, or
    3. The note is a barely audible "ghost" note (note in standard notation is also in parentheses).

GUITAR BIBLES
from  HAL•LEONARD®

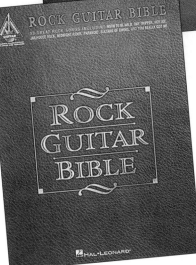

Hal Leonard proudly presents the Guitar Bible series. Each volume contains great songs in authentic, note-for-note transcriptions with lyrics and tablature.

ACOUSTIC GUITAR BIBLE
35 acoustic classics: Angie • Building a Mystery • Change the World • Dust in the Wind • Hold My Hand • Iris • Maggie May • Southern Cross • Tears in Heaven • Wild World • and more.
00690432...$19.95

ACOUSTIC ROCK GUITAR BIBLE
35 classics: And I Love Her • Behind Blue Eyes • Come to My Window • Free Fallin' • Give a Little Bit • More Than Words • Night Moves • Pink Houses • Slide • 3 AM • and more.
00690625...$19.95

BLUES GUITAR BIBLE
35 blues tunes: Boom Boom • Hide Away • I Can't Quit You Baby • I'm Your Hoochie Coochie Man • Killing Floor • Pride and Joy • Sweet Little Angel • The Thrill Is Gone • and more.
00690437...$19.95

BLUES-ROCK GUITAR BIBLE
35 songs: Cross Road Blues (Crossroads) • Hide Away • The House Is Rockin' • Love Struck Baby • Move It On Over • Piece of My Heart • Statesboro Blues • You Shook Me • more.
00690450...$19.95

CLASSIC ROCK GUITAR BIBLE
33 essential rock songs: Beast of Burden • Cat Scratch Fever • Double Vision • Free Ride • Hard to Handle • Life in the Fast Lane • The Stroke • Won't Get Fooled Again • and more.
00690662...$19.95

COUNTRY GUITAR BIBLE
35 country classics: Ain't Goin' Down • Blue Eyes Crying in the Rain • Boot Scootin' Boogie • Friends in Low Places • I'm So Lonesome I Could Cry • T-R-O-U-B-L-E • and more.
00690465...$19.95

DISCO GUITAR BIBLE
30 stand-out songs from the disco days: Brick House • Disco Inferno • Funkytown • Get Down Tonight • I Love the Night Life • Le Freak • Stayin' Alive • Y.M.C.A. • and more.
00690627...$17.95

EARLY ROCK GUITAR BIBLE
35 fantastic classics: Blue Suede Shoes • Do Wah Diddy Diddy • Hang On Sloopy • I'm a Believer • Louie, Louie • Oh, Pretty Woman • Surfin' U.S.A. • Twist and Shout • and more.
00690680...$17.95

FOLK-ROCK GUITAR BIBLE
35 songs: At Seventeen • Blackbird • Fire and Rain • Happy Together • Leaving on a Jet Plane • Our House • Time in a Bottle • Turn! Turn! Turn! • You've Got a Friend • more.
00690464...$19.95

GRUNGE GUITAR BIBLE
30 songs: All Apologies • Counting Blue Cars • Glycerine • Jesus Christ Pose • Lithium • Man in the Box • Nearly Lost You • Smells like Teen Spirit • This Is a Call • Violet • and more.
00690649...$19.95

HARD ROCK GUITAR BIBLE
35 songs: Ballroom Blitz • Bang a Gong • Barracuda • Living After Midnight • Rock You like a Hurricane • School's Out • Welcome to the Jungle • You Give Love a Bad Name • more.
00690453...$22.99

JAZZ GUITAR BIBLE
31 songs: Body and Soul • In a Sentimental Mood • My Funny Valentine • Nuages • Satin Doll • So What • Star Dust • Take Five • Tangerine • Yardbird Suite • and more.
00690466...$19.95

POP/ROCK GUITAR BIBLE
35 pop hits: Change the World • Heartache Tonight • Money for Nothing • Mony, Mony • Pink Houses • Smooth • Summer of '69 • 3 AM • What I Like About You • and more.
00690517...$19.95

PROGRESSIVE ROCK GUITAR BIBLE
28 great art-rock and metal tunes: Astronomy Domine • Empire • Eyes of a Stranger • Ghost of Karelia • Lavender • Lucky Man • Money • Monument • Rhythm of Love • The Story in Your Eyes • Strange Magic • Turn It On Again • 21st Century Schizoid Man • The Wall • and more.
00690626...$19.99

R&B GUITAR BIBLE
35 R&B classics: Brick House • Fire • I Got You (I Feel Good) • Love Rollercoaster • Shining Star • Sir Duke • Super Freak • and more.
00690452...$19.95

ROCK BASS BIBLE
35 rock bass hits: Another One Bites the Dust • Come Together • Fat Bottomed Girls • I Want You to Want Me • Miss You • Suffragette City • Sweet Emotion • White Room • You Shook Me • more!
00690446...$19.95

ROCK GUITAR BIBLE
33 songs: All Day and All of the Night • Born to Be Wild • Day Tripper • Hey Joe • Jailhouse Rock • Money • Paranoid • Sultans of Swing • Walk This Way • You Really Got Me • more!
00690313...$19.95

ROCKABILLY GUITAR BIBLE
31 songs from artists such as Elvis, Buddy Holly and the Brian Setzer Orchestra: Blue Suede Shoes • Hello Mary Lou • Peggy Sue • Rock This Town • Travelin' Man • and more.
00690570...$19.95

SOUTHERN ROCK GUITAR BIBLE
25 southern rock classics: Can't You See • Free Bird • Hold On Loosely • La Grange • Midnight Rider • Sweet Home Alabama • and more.
00690723...$19.95

Prices, contents, and availability subject to change without notice.

FOR MORE INFORMATION, SEE YOUR LOCAL MUSIC DEALER, OR WRITE TO:

 HAL•LEONARD® CORPORATION
7777 W. BLUEMOUND RD. P.O. BOX 13819 MILWAUKEE, WI 53213

Visit Hal Leonard online at **www.halleonard.com**

GUITAR RECORDED VERSIONS®

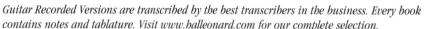

Guitar Recorded Versions® are note-for-note transcriptions of guitar music taken directly off recordings. This series, one of the most popular in print today, features some of the greatest guitar players and groups from blues and rock to country and jazz.

Guitar Recorded Versions are transcribed by the best transcribers in the business. Every book contains notes and tablature. Visit www.halleonard.com for our complete selection.

AUTHENTIC TRANSCRIPTIONS WITH NOTES AND TABLATURE

AUTHENTIC TRANSCRIPTIONS
WITH NOTES AND TABLATURE

FOR MORE INFORMATION, SEE YOUR LOCAL MUSIC DEALER,
OR WRITE TO:

7777 W. BLUEMOUND RD. P.O. BOX 13819 MILWAUKEE, WI 53213

Complete songlists and more at www.halleonard.com
Prices, contents, and availability subject to change without notice.

0611

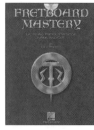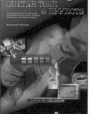